GEORGE SAITOH

BELLE ISLE

plays by the same author

COWARD'S SOUP

MOSS

PLAY THE ADVANTAGE

L'IL HAT

HOLD STILL

THE SNUGBARON

novels

ALL THE DEAD ANIMALS

GEORGE SAITOH

BELLE ISLE

a five-act play

Janus Creations

2017

"Things which offend when present, and affright,
In memory, well painted, move delight."

—Abraham Cowley

'"Do you love me? Believe me, you don't love me. Believe
me. You don't love anyone. How could you? And noone
loves you. How could they? Except me. It's only because I
love you that I'm telling you all this...I love you. Believe
me...Well don't believe me because I say so!" That's my
mother.'

—RD Laing

Copyright © 2017 by George Saitoh

All rights reserved

ISBN-13: 978-0-9987840-0-7

ISBN-10: 0-9987840-0-1

Library of Congress Control Number: 2017935904

NOTE ON THE TEXT

BELLE ISLE was first performed in public as a rehearsed reading in August 2014 at The New Theatre in Dublin using this text.

David (adult) **Harry**	Rob Wallace
Psychotherapist **Vincent the Liar** **Aubrey Wills** **Frank**	Ciaran Mooney
Joanne (adult David's wife) **Mary** **Lusty**	Yvonne Murphy
Harry Jr. **Salty** **Teenager in ditch**	Seán Mac Mathúna
David (boy) **Hago**	Dan Frawley
Joanne (boy David's sister) **Bridie** **Workman**	Róisín Hunt
Stage directions	Mary-Bridget Donnelly
Director	Paul Doran

CHARACTERS

Harry, *45 years old unemployed man*

Mary, *45 years old, wife of Harry*

Harry Jr., *14 years old son of Harry and Mary*

Frank, *40 years old brother of Harry, and a single parent*

Joanne, *14 years old daughter of Frank*

David (boy), *7 years old son of Frank*

Hago, *17 years old gang leader*

Lusty, *15 years old female gang member*

Salty, *17 years old gang member*

Gang member 1, *aged 15-17*

Gang member 2, *aged 15-17*

Gang member 3, *aged 15-17*

David (adult), *aged 27*

Joanne (adult David's wife), *aged 32*

Aubrey, *35 years old businessman*

Psychotherapist, *aged 55*

Kevin, *7 years old boy with glasses*

Party kid 1, *aged 7*

Party kid 2, *aged 7*

Party kid 3, *aged 7*

Bridie, *60 years old relation of Harry, lives alone*

Young mother, *30 years old*

3 young girls, *aged 7-11*

Workman A, *aged 20-40*

Workman B, *aged 20-40*

Workman C, *aged 20-40*

Workman D, *aged 20-40*

Workman E, *aged 20-40*

Boy A (apprentice), *aged 14*

Vincent the Liar, *a ghost, aged 55 (to double as psychotherapist)*

Teenager in ditch, *aged 14*

Catholic priest, *aged 50*

PASSION SPEAKS FOR US

Deeply impressed
by my willingness
to go on
I put the mystery
down to this being
a lovely island

mercurial seasons
sun-weathered surfaces
coming to luster
impatient gusts throwing
heads of flowers
into tumult

distracted, my mistaken
involvement takes score
marks points on a board

levers rocks
rocks lever

saved

for another while.

ACT I

Scene 1

Joanne is in the kitchen of her house in Dublin. She is seeing a small man, her husband's friend John Brown, whom she does not like, out the door.

JOANNE: Goodbye John. I'll tell him to call you as soon as he comes in.

Closes the door and goes about her business in the kitchen. In a few moments Joanne's husband, David, enters the house.

JOANNE: Is everything all right?

DAVID: Yeah, why?

JOANNE: No, I was just wondering, that's all. Your little pal was just here looking for you.

DAVID: Who?

JOANNE: The little guy, what's his name again?

DAVID: John Brown?

JOANNE: That's him I think. I could be mistaken but I could have sworn he was acting a bit strange.

DAVID: In what way?

JOANNE: I don't know. It's hard to say. But there was something struck me as peculiar about his manner. It caught my attention. (*Joanne hardly knows John Brown.*) It was like he was...em...

DAVID: Like he was what?

JOANNE: I don't know. I could be wrong now, it wouldn't be the first time (*laughs*) of course. But I have to say—and I'm usually good at spotting this kind of thing in people—I have to say...

DAVID: (*impatiently*). Go on and say it! What was it you thought he was like?

JOANNE: (*offended*). Well, what I was trying to tell you about your little pal, John Brown, if only you'd have the courtesy to let the other person finish a sentence off—I'm only making conversation with you by the way, there's no need for you to always jump on the defensive every time I mention one of your pals...

DAVID: I'm not jumping on the defensive!

JOANNE: Oh, right.

Suddenly calm, turns her head aside and sniffs, rubs her nose with a knuckle twice.

DAVID: (*calming himself down forcibly*). What was strange about John Brown?

JOANNE: (*goes about her business. Sniffs*).

DAVID: What was it? Tell me.

JOANNE: (*looks at him defiantly. Sniffs*).

DAVID: (*pathetically*). Please, I need to know.

JOANNE: Well, if you must know—and I should know better by now than to be giving my senses to the likes of you, it always comes back to bite me in the arse...(*she pauses here to watch the submission in his eyes, to see if he will dare to rise again)*...If you must know—and again this is only my impression, and I always trust my impressions of people, though God knows how often they've gotten me into trouble, even when they've turned out to be true...*(David is struggling not to lose his temper. She is watching him like a hawk as she presses on)*...in the fullness of time. I should probably keep my mouth shut and say nothing and let you all get on with it.

DAVID: No. You can't do that. People have to hear what you think.

JOANNE: Evidently not you anyway.

DAVID: Of course I do.

JOANNE: It doesn't seem like it from your attitude. Why is it so hard for people to listen to one another these days? Why does there have to be so much aggression and evasion all the time? Can you answer that simple question for me?

DAVID: *(stumped. Shakes his head).*

JOANNE: You see I grew up in an atmosphere of aggression, where nobody spoke unless they were threatened or tricked, where words were used like ammunition—not to express thoughts or feelings but to annihilate another person. Now, I know you're laughing at me as I say this to you but I don't care.

DAVID: I'm not laughing.

JOANNE: Well, I could name a list of people who would be laughing at me if they were here now, I can assure you. But fuck them! I don't care, I'm going to say what I think regardless of them, even if it kills me or leaves me friendless until the day of my death, so help me God.

DAVID: That's never going to happen.

JOANNE: Mark my words. It would be just my luck to be a victim of my own good intentions. I ought to just say fuck it like everyone else does. I'm serious. I'd be within my rights. Why should I care so much about things if nobody else does? And get myself laughed at behind my back for trying to do the right thing? Hah? Answer me that, hah?

DAVID: (*no answer).*

JOANNE: Hah?

DAVID: You shouldn't worry about that.

JOANNE: What do you mean? Shouldn't worry about what?

DAVID: About being laughed at.

JOANNE: (*looks like a slapped child).*

DAVID: I mean, nobody laughs at you behind your back. It's all in your head.

JOANNE: Do you?

DAVID: Of course not!

JOANNE: But you don't always believe what I tell you is true.

DAVID: Of course I do.

JOANNE: Then why, after I've told you something I know
           happened, do you make me feel like a little liar?
           Like a child who is making up tales?

DAVID: I don't!

JOANNE: *(looks at him with utter contempt).* Are you
           telling me what I do or do not feel? Are you able
           to do that? Well, then. Let me tell you a little
           story about telling other people what they are
           feeling...

DAVID: No! Of course not, that's not what I meant. I'm
           sorry. What I meant to say was that I didn't
           mean to make you feel that way.

JOANNE: You didn't mean to make me feel that way? Well
           what way did you mean to make me feel?

DAVID: What I mean is I had no idea what way I was
           making you feel. I never even thought about it.

JOANNE: You never even thought about it. Well, do you
           ever think about it?

DAVID: *(silence).*

JOANNE: Do you ever think about how you make me feel,
           hah?

DAVID: *(struggling to answer).*

JOANNE: Answer me that much at least. Do you ever
           think about how I feel?

DAVID: Of course I think about how you feel.

JOANNE: When?

DAVID: What?

JOANNE: When? Give me an example.

DAVID: *(silence)*.

JOANNE: Give me one example.

DAVID: *(silence)*.

JOANNE: Hah? One example.

DAVID: Well do you ever think about how I feel?

JOANNE: *(sinisterly calm)*. All the time.

DAVID: Then give me one example.

JOANNE: Didn't I ask you when you walked in the door is everything alright?

DAVID: So what?

JOANNE: Didn't I say I was 'just wondering'?

DAVID: So what?

JOANNE: What do you think I was wondering about?

DAVID: *(silence)*.

JOANNE: About how you might be feeling! I told you something struck me as strange about John Brown, didn't I, hah?

DAVID: *(silence, anger rising)*.

JOANNE: And so I suspected it had something to do with you, that it might be a source of anxiety in you, so I wanted to give you a chance to tell me first. IF YOU WANTED TO! But I didn't want to crowd you, so I kept my mouth shut to give you a chance to tell me yourself. In your own way!

And now look what's happened! Do you see what happens to me for caring about other people? For being considerate? How it's all one-way traffic? How it's always misconstrued?

DAVID: *(silence).*

JOANNE: I don't know. Maybe I'm wasting my breath again as usual. No one listens to a word I say. 'Joanne, shut the fuck up will you. Joanne, big mouth Joanne, always talking about her feelings and boring everybody with them. Avoid Joanne at all costs, she talks too much.' Yeah, well maybe other people talk too little! How about that, hah?

DAVID: *(silence).*

JOANNE: What do you say to that? Isn't it possible that everyone around here talks too little? That that's what the problem is? That if everyone could only feel a little freer about saying what was in their hearts, that the world would be a better place, with less aggression, less anger and threats, hah?

DAVID: *(silence).*

JOANNE: You don't think so?

DAVID: I do.

JOANNE: Oh, you do think so. Well, thank you for granting me that much at least.

DAVID: *(silence).*

JOANNE: Anyway, so much for John fucking Brown.

Pause.

DAVID: (*notices a package on the floor for the first time*). What's that over there?

JOANNE: What's what?

DAVID: That thing there.

JOANNE: Oh that thing. It's something John Brown dropped off for you.

DAVID: For me? Why didn't you tell me?

JOANNE: Now hold on a fucking minute there. Don't go raising your voice to me again. We've been through this already. I won't go through it all again. I just told you what it is, didn't I? If you'd given me a chance to speak I'd have told you when you came in, instead of jumping all over me like you did. You're lucky I didn't dance on it and trample it to pieces, whatever it is, instead of being your errand girl. What do you take me for at all, hah? Do you think I'm here to take messages and packages for you, and abuse on top of it? Well you can think again. I'm telling you now, I've had enough of being treated as a skivvy by people; those days are well and truly over.

DAVID: (*retrieves the package and opens it*).

JOANNE: (*watching him with intense interest*). I've had enough codswallop from people to last me a lifetime. (*David begins opening the package. She leans in, greedy to discover what it is.*) It'll probably explain the strange attitude John

Brown had when he delivered it. Well, at least that will put to rest one mystery.

DAVID: What mystery?

JOANNE: The mystery of why John Brown seemed strange.

DAVID: How do you know he was strange? You hardly know him!

JOANNE: I know people.

DAVID: You haven't said how he was strange. Maybe I wouldn't have thought there was anything strange about him.

JOANNE: How do you know? You weren't even there when he came in with that thing under one arm and his other arm in a sling.

DAVID: In a sling? (*He stops opening the package.*) What do you mean?

JOANNE: In a sling. What do you think I mean? What's in there will probably explain why.

DAVID: (*gritting his teeth, he goes back to opening the package. It's wrapped in multiple layers like 'pass the parcel'. He stops again*). Is that what was strange about him, the sling?

JOANNE: (*adopts a sudden playfulness, setting herself apart from the world of problems where David remains*). Oh no. No, it wasn't that. There was something else about him that was strange.

DAVID: What was it?

JOANNE: What?

DAVID: *(raising his voice)*. What was it?

JOANNE: I don't know. Something about the way he behaved towards the other two. Something...

DAVID: The other two? What other two?

JOANNE: The two that accompanied him to the door.

DAVID: Why didn't you tell me about...all right forget that. Did you recognize any of the other two?

JOANNE: *(flippantly)*. No.

DAVID: Well, did you?

JOANNE: *(smiling)*. Noooo...

DAVID: *(thinks for a while)*.

JOANNE: *(watching him slyly, very carefully)*. What is it then?

DAVID: *(looks at her furiously. He continues to open the package. As he does so he becomes aware of her eagerness to see his reaction to the contents. He slows down and then stops)*.

JOANNE: What's wrong?

DAVID: *(silence)*.

JOANNE: Why aren't you opening it? What's the matter? ...What?... Are you afraid of what you'll find?

DAVID: *(silence)*.

JOANNE: For fuck's sake, I don't know! After all this and then you won't even open it!

DAVID: *(silence. He gets up as if to go away but stalls, looks confused, turns around, tries to think.*

Joanne is watching him all the time).

JOANNE: Open it! I don't know why anyone bothers with you. No wonder you have everyone confused all the time. What are you doing now?

DAVID: *(silence. He looks at her, he grows angry at himself for not being able to think clearly, at the sound of her voice).*

JOANNE: *(looking at him like he's a disobedient child).* Well, do something for fuck's sake! Don't just stand there in the middle of the floor like a spare prick holding that thing in your...

DAVID: Argghhh!

He smashes the package on the floor beside her feet. Its contents are shattered.

JOANNE: Look what you've done now!

DAVID: You crazy bitch, I'll kill you.

He lunges and grabs her by the throat. She starts screaming. He beats her and she falls to the floor. Then he goes out, leaving her sobbing. After David leaves Joanne controls herself and crawls to look at the scraps of broken material. She picks them up and tries to piece together whatever it was.

JOANNE: What is it? A bottle? A bottle of what? There's no liquid. An empty bottle? He did all this over an empty...what are these things, pieces of wood? Some kind of a toy...it's a toy ship or something...what's this thing...

Pause.

...it's a ship in a bottle. A ship in a bottle. He did all this for the sake of a stupid ship in a bottle. He beat me up over a silly ship in a bottle. (*She sits back and breaks down in tears again, genuinely feeling sorry for herself, the ordeal of her life.*) It's one of those poxy things his father used to make and give away to people. We even have one here ourselves, over there in the corner. (*Looks over, gets up and goes over to look for it*) It used to be here in the corner gathering dust. I hated the sight of the thing but he insisted on keeping it. I don't know how many times I asked him to get rid of it. (*Looks in the corner but cannot find it.*) Now where is it gone? He must have moved it.

Joanne cleans up the mess. She then starts to pull out all of the kitchen utensils from the cupboards and wash them along with the cabinets and cooker. She takes out a range of cleaning fluids and cloths. After a while, David returns, enters sheepishly.

DAVID: Leave them. I'll do them.

JOANNE: *(washing furiously).* It's all right. They're almost done now.

Pause.

DAVID: *(coming closer).* Here, let me do the rest.

JOANNE: *(snapping).* I'll finish them myself I told you!

She looks at him sideways.

DAVID: (*backing off, goes behind her and watches her back. He can see her struggling to resist turning around to look at him. Instead, she does something to her right or left and it allows her to glance sideways at him*). Listen...

JOANNE: Don't!

DAVID: I have to tell you something.

JOANNE: I don't want to hear.

DAVID: I'm nothing...

JOANNE: (*look of disgust*). What?

DAVID: I mean I'm not in control...

JOANNE: You most certainly are not in control...

DAVID: No, what I mean is I'm not in control of my feelings.

JOANNE: What the fuck do you mean 'I'm not in control of my feelings?' Well then who is?

DAVID: It's not that I'm not in control...

JOANNE: It's NOT that you're not in control?

DAVID: No, it's just that...

JOANNE: Are you saying you're crazy?

DAVID: (*thinks about this—it wasn't what he wanted to say but it might be a way out*). I'm not sure. Sometimes I might be.

JOANNE: Well, what are you going to do about it?

DAVID: What?

JOANNE: I can't have your craziness hanging over me all

the time, wondering when it's going to erupt again. You better go and sort yourself out.

DAVID: How?

JOANNE: That's your business.

Turns back to the washing up.

Pause.

DAVID: I remember when my father used to…

JOANNE: *(stops washing).* I don't want to hear all this again ok! Enough about your father! From what you've told me about him you're the very same as your father was. Like father like son.

Resumes vigorous washing.

DAVID: *(silence).*

JOANNE: I don't think I can take any more of this.

DAVID: I'm sorry.

JOANNE: I really don't.

DAVID: I'm so sorry.

JOANNE: You say that every time. But it's not good enough.

DAVID: But sometimes…

JOANNE: Sometimes what?

DAVID: Sometimes it's not all my fault.

JOANNE: *(turns on him sharply).* Not your fault? Not your fault that you go crazy and abuse me? How can that not be your fault? Is it your father's fault?

DAVID: No.

JOANNE: Is it your mother's?

DAVID: (*silence*).

JOANNE: Then whose is it?

DAVID: (*silence*).

JOANNE: Is it mine?

DAVID: Well...

JOANNE: Well what you crazy bastard! Are you trying to tell me that I asked to be abused by you, that I ASK for it?

DAVID: No.

JOANNE: Well then what?

DAVID: Not exactly.

JOANNE: Not exactly? What the fuck does that mean? Either I do or I don't, it can't be two ways. Come out with it straight! At least have the guts to tell me what you think to my face!

DAVID: (*silence*).

JOANNE: If you were man enough to tell me your feelings I wouldn't have to be a mind reader all the time. We wouldn't have all these games.

DAVID: (*silence*).

JOANNE: Do you not see where all this secrecy between us leads to, hah? Or are you completely blind to that as well?

DAVID: (*silence*).

JOANNE: We can't go on with all these ridiculous secrets, it leads to suspicion and distrust—and if we can't trust each other enough to tell each other everything then who can we trust? Your family? At least, whatever their faults, we can rely on my family if I had to, but I don't ever want to have to! I want to be self-reliant! And I need somebody who can understand that. I've always been self-reliant. Ever since I can remember I was out finding ways to earn a few bob, little odd jobs wherever I could find them. Out working, cleaning and scrubbing. (*Gets to work again on the dishes, goes silent for a moment*). But I suppose it's too much to ask that somebody like me wouldn't be taken advantage of. I thought you might have been different from the rest of them.

DAVID: (*wretchedly tries to take a pot from her*).

JOANNE: Go away from me!

               Starts to cry.

DAVID: (*puts his arms around her. She lets him. He hugs her and she allows it*).

JOANNE: (*sobbing*). Sometimes I do get very tired.

DAVID: I know.

JOANNE: Sometimes I just wish I could take a long sleep.

DAVID: I know.

JOANNE: (*bitterly*). I wouldn't mind but I had a wonderful day yesterday. I should have known it was too good to last.

DAVID: Come here.

JOANNE: You don't realize what you do to me. How it upsets me when you turn on me. It's like the past coming back again to haunt me. I'm like a helpless little girl again under somebody's control. It's like I've achieved nothing since then. I swore I'd never allow myself to take that from any man.

DAVID: I'm sorry.

JOANNE: You really must get yourself sorted out, or we can't go on. Your moods have to be brought under control some way. I don't know how— either by medication or therapy. But something has to be done about this. I don't see why I should suffer another day because of problems from your past. I have enough from my own.

DAVID: I know. I'll have to do something.

JOANNE: Otherwise how can we start a family and give our children the love and stability every child needs to grow up into a healthy and happy adult?

Both stare into space and contemplate their private fears and hopes.

Scene 2

Some months later. A psychotherapist's salon. David is lying on a high couch like a corpse on a mortuary slab. The soles of his feet are facing the audience, his head raised slightly above them. The psychologist, a man of 55, is sitting beside him. A lamp gives the room a sumptuous luster.

DAVID: Joanne wants a baby. She'd been threatening for a while to leave me if we don't have one. Then the other night, out of the blue, she said she was going to leave. I wanted to kill her. When I finally fell asleep I had a strange dream. Derek McGann was in it. He was moving rapidly between Africa and Ireland, coming and going at all hours of the night. In Africa he kept dogs, crazed dogs that were only calm when he was around them. He'd throw blankets over them to play with them when he came home late at night, and then he'd feed them. Ireland was where he spent his days, working. Wreaking revenge.

THERAPIST: Were you present in the dream?

DAVID: I think so but I'm not a hundred percent sure it was me. There were moments when I wasn't aware of Derek and it seemed to be my hands that were doing things.

Pause.

THERAPIST: What kind of things?

DAVID: Killing people.

THERAPIST: The way that Derek was killing people?

Pause.

DAVID: I didn't see Derek killing anybody. I just know that's what he was doing, by the way he was with the dogs afterwards when he came back—they were the only thing that could calm him down, the only thing he looked forward to or had any interest in, and it seemed they had to be crazed into the bargain. I knew he was killing people by his eyes. They moved slowly and were narrowed and small—the opposite of wide open with wonder. His eyes showed something like anti-wonder. That's the best way I can describe it to you. Like a return from wonder—eyes that had found too much wonder elsewhere, more than they had been able to take in.

Pause.

THERAPIST: What people did you kill?

DAVID: I told you I'm not sure it was me in the dream. It's possible that I was Derek at those times, that I became him and that's why he was not visible to me in those parts of the dream.

Pause.

I killed my mother…I mean Mary who's really my aunt… and all of her friends and their families. I found them all together in a room on the upper floor of a 4 or 5 story building, like a hotel. They were having some kind of a gathering, a gloomy party where everyone sat round drinking soup with nothing to say, like a pack of guilty convicts in a waiting room.

THERAPIST: Guilty?

DAVID: They all had an air of guilt about them, waiting for something to happen to them that wasn't going to be pleasant, but might come as a relief…so they weren't terrified, only gloomy with uncertainty. They were all there, my mother's friends. One of them, the one who wanted to be a priest, was sitting there in drag. Her friends Maeve and Clem were there, and all their children. My mother, was sitting right behind Maeve, moving her head in sync with the other's— both heads only a few inches apart, my mother's head hiding behind the other. All the rest of them were scattered throughout the room. The room was all red plush and black.

THERAPIST: Was your father there?

DAVID: You mean my uncle Harry? No, he wasn't there, or anyone connected with him.

Pause.

They all looked up when I entered, though none of them registered surprise or much interest. Certainly no fear. It was as if I was not who they were expecting, and although I could stay if I really wanted to, I was not particularly welcome. Some of them, the children and younger adults especially, seemed to sneer at me, wanting to show me they knew something. One of them flashed me her tit. The older ones ignored me. None of them looked worried. Except my mother—from what I could see of her behind Maeve's big head. But then my mother always looked worried and cowed among her own friends if I was there.

Pause.

I went over and killed her first.

Pause.

I killed Maeve next but it was important for me to kill my mother first and separately, to isolate her out because that was the very thing that she always avoided in life—being separate, being a person of her own, a person who stood for something, somebody you could go to.

Pause.

THERAPIST: How did you kill them?

DAVID: I shot them. First I asked them each a

question they couldn't answer. Then I shot them. One by one.

Pause.

David looks at the Psychotherapist, his mouth starts masticating.

THERAPIST: What questions did you ask them?

DAVID: I don't remember. But I know they couldn't answer them.

THERAPIST: Were they shot for failing to answer the question?

DAVID: Yes and no.

THERAPIST: What does that mean?

Pause.

David's face flushes with rage, and he flashes the Psychotherapist a hateful look. He calms down.

DAVID: I mean I made it seem that way.

Pause.

But it wasn't how it really was. I was going to kill them whether they answered me or not, but I didn't tell them that. I offered them a little bit of false hope. To test their humanity. As I expected they hadn't the courage to reach for it. The rats that they are they couldn't see anything in life except death waiting for them. They were always on their way to death, I now realized after entering that room. What I did was help them along on their way.

Pause.

THERAPIST: How did killing them make you feel?

DAVID: Tired. Tired and annoyed with myself for taking so long to do it. And stupid as well.

THERAPIST: Stupid?

DAVID: I felt stupid.

THERAPIST: Omnipotence doesn't often go hand in hand with stupidity. Why do you think you felt stupid?

DAVID: I don't know why.

Pause.

THERAPIST: Could if be that you felt stupid for not being able to design a more ingenious way of hurting them, that the way you chose might have been playing into their hands and granting their wishes above and beyond your own?

Pause.

DAVID: Maybe. It was like shooting diseased rabbits. It wasn't as gratifying as taking their lives should have been. They didn't even care that their own family members were being culled, or that their turn was coming up next. They just sat and waited like schoolchildren.

THERAPIST: Like schoolchildren?

DAVID: That's what they reminded me of when I produced the gun. Sitting there in their seats, each with their own separate table, except my mother of course who sat behind Maeve. All sitting there in silence with their eyes looking up at the teacher who was going to do exactly what pleased him, and they were going to accept it from him.

           Pause.

THERAPIST: How did the dream end?

DAVID: After they were killed I went to Africa, to find Derek. I had to talk to him. I had to tell him that I had found somebody like him, somebody who went out and avenged himself on people. I was excited by the prospect of telling him, of coming to such a perfect understanding with another person, of being able to say without doubt that I knew another person's life, why they did the things they did, lived the way they lived, because they had to live that way. Because there was no other way for them to live. And I wanted to sympathize with him.

           Pause.

THERAPIST: Did you find him?

DAVID: Yeah. I found him.

THERAPIST: What was his reaction to what you told him?

           Pause.

DAVID: He didn't care.

Pause.

He just went on playing with his dogs until it was time for him to go back to Ireland again.

Pause.

THERAPIST: How did that make you feel?

Pause.

DAVID: Like trying again...Like having another crack at killing, in another way that was more gratifying. I felt like I'd botched the last massacre. I wanted another chance to do it right.

THERAPIST: How would you do it if you had another chance?

DAVID: I don't know...more slowly...more playfully. I'd give them a little pleasure along the way to trick more truth out of them. A stroke of a feather on the cheek, a syringe of honey into their mouth, a tweak of a nipple. Show them a photo of their parents. Give them a range of false options to distract their thoughts. I don't know. So many things come to mind all of a sudden, all the things I could have tried instead of wasting the opportunity by just asking a simple question.

Pause.

THERAPIST: How do you think you would profit from such killing?

DAVID: I'd get to know them finally. I'd extract the truth about them, the filthy truth from their hearts and find out what's really in there.

Pause.

(His eyes shine with passion and hope.)

I would confirm all my suspicions! I would give them no more places to hide and deceive me from. I would have a chance to discover secrets about them that even they are not aware of. I would show them up, at last, for what they truly are and be satisfied that I had witnessed before my own eyes what my instincts had tormented me with all along, for which I had no proof. I could prove they were no good, show them the reason they were no good, and then finish them off. So they would be no good no longer. Something we could all agree on.

Pause.

Killing my mother's friends and their families had proved nothing really, nothing that I didn't have proof enough of already. It didn't bring out those terrible human secrets... the humiliatable heart's contents were left intact...undisturbed... unhumiliated. I gave each of them a *coup de grace* they didn't deserve.

Pause.

That's probably why Derek took no notice of

me. This 'person' I had found for him, that was supposed to be so like Derek, was not like him at all—not in Derek's judgment...only in the judgment of someone who didn't understand anything. Someone who judged all killing and all killers to be the same. As people who were just taking revenge. But they weren't all the same, some were...some of them were...artists...the rest just...just imitators.

Pause.

Derek killed for knowledge...about life and death. The way some people write books or make films. Like them, he got directly to the knowledge he needed every time, only much faster. He came straight to the only knowledge that matters. Knowledge of fear. When it comes down to it all that matters is fear. Derek knew that better than anyone else. And his knowledge of fear was pure.

Curtain

ACT II

Scene 1

Twenty years earlier in a field with a ditch. A winter's night.
We hear various noises, a distant sound of gunfire and the
faraway drone of a 2-stroke motorcycle. A dirty white plastic
fertilizer bag on the ground shifts intermittently. There is a
milk carton and charred objects and ashes alongside the bag.
A cow moos and it is followed by the voice of teenager
ranting in his sleep, beginning and ending incoherently.

TEENAGER: I wasn't. I swear I wasn't. I wasn't. I swear to
you on my life I wasn't. I'm telling you. I
wasn't! I swear to you! I wasn't. I
wasn't!!...no, please!

The bag is kicked violently and he sits up. He
looks around him, takes his bearings and
catches his breath. He checks the fasteners on
his coat, pulls the plastic bag up as far as it
will go and settles back down again. Soon he
starts to move again as before.

Enter Harry with a shotgun and a large hand
lamp, which he uses to pan the field. With him
is his nephew David. David is holding a dead
rabbit by the hind legs. They move stealthily
and then stop abruptly. Harry pans the field
with the shotgun leveled against the lamp

handle. The lamp stops at a point and Harry leans down and puts a hand on David's arm and David looks to where the lamp is aimed. David nods and whispers.

DAVID: I see it.

Slowly, very slowly, Harry raises the gun to his shoulder while keeping the beam fixed on the spot. At the edge of the stage Vincent the Liar appears.

VINCENT: *(to the audience).* He is crying out for the touch of another human being.

(Harry takes aim, then drops the gun a fraction from his shoulder. He glances at David and adjusts the lamp to a nearby point. He then rapidly puts the gun to his shoulder and fires. Bang! The barrel kicks up and the beam along with it. At the sound of gunshot, a scream is heard from the teenager behind them who curls up in a ball. David leaps in fright, jolts the rabbit about, and both he and Harry turn to see who is behind them. In the distance we hear the squeals of a rabbit, shot but still alive.)

He will enter a softer world.

Harry fumbles with the lamp to shine it at the source of the human voice. He extends an arm and uses it to sweep David behind him. Harry looks for a while, until he understands what he sees. The squealing of the rabbit ebbs away. David tries to anticipate Harry's reaction.

HARRY: Do you want a smoke?

He drops the beam to his side.

TEENAGER: *(no reply, some unfurling).*

HARRY: Here.

(He produces a box and a lighter from his pocket and holds it out. The teenager slowly unfurls. Harry moves his arm up and down.)

Here. Take them.

David appears and the teenager sees him, unfurls some more, sees the rabbit and relaxes. Harry allows him time to take it all in. The teenager reaches out his hand. Harry steps in closer and bends a knee, like a genuflection, and hands over the cigarettes and matches.

TEENAGER: *(to David).* That's a nice one you got.

DAVID: *(holding up the rabbit).* It was a headshot.

TEENAGER: It'll make a nice soup so.

HARRY: *(putting a hand on David's shoulder).*

It sure will.

All three remain together in silence. The teenager lights a cigarette.

HARRY: Good luck.

TEENAGER: Good luck. Thanks.

Harry and David go on their way. Vincent the Liar disappears.

Scene 2

The following afternoon. Harry is outside his house. The lower half of the house has boarded up windows. The wall and boards are covered in graffiti: DOMO, MICKA, BULLET, UP THE RA, FUCK THE QUEEN, a drawing of 2 Vs interlocked and genitalia between them. The upper level has one open window. Harry is listening carefully for something, walking to and fro, straining to hear. Pavarotti comes faintly from the open window and arouses a chirping bird somewhere.

Harry: *(speaking up to the window).* Turn it up a bit Mary, would you?

                           Pavarotti grows louder. The birdsong grows louder. There is a look of glee on Harry's face as he walks around the listening for the bird. Suddenly he sees something in the distance and his mood abruptly changes. He goes back inside. The upper window is closed. In a few moments a gang of youths saunter past. Hago, the gang leader, has a dead sparrow hawk in a clear plastic bag. Each of others holds something in their hand: a stick, a car aerial, a cosh, a bridle for a horse. As they walk past the house the upper window re-opens and Harry brandishes a shotgun, aiming it at the head of Hago. Hago doesn't stop or even look up but continues sauntering slowly on, the barrel of the gun following him.

When he stops the group gathers around him, sitting on the ground outside the house. Some of them start picking at the ground. Hago goes to the wall of the house directly beneath Harry, bends down and puts a finger in a crack. We hear the urgent sound of chirping. The gang members glance up at Harry and laugh.

HAGO: Blue tits it looks like.

(*He turns round to search all over the stage with his eyes.*) Where's the mother I wonder. (*Lusty laughs loudly. The others look all around, Harry too.*) There she is over there, look. (*They all look at a woman in the audience.*)

Pause.

There's nothing to worry about.

Harry's arms go limp, his shoulders sag. There seems to be an exciting new smell in the air: the smell of linseed oil-impregnated combat fatigues. Hago raises the bag with the dead sparrow hawk and waves it around. He laughs. The rest of the gang join in the laughter as Harry retreats into the house and closes the window. The gang settles and prepares a fire. One of them has a bag of sugar.

HAGO: Where's the sugar?

LUSTY: Salty?

HAGO: Where's the sugar?

MEMBER A: Salty has it!

SALTY: *(handing over the sugar).* The only way to
                 light wet wood. I told you!

                 *They don't say much. They examine the
                 ground, digging up stones and bottle caps.
                 Among them Hago looks noble. From inside
                 the house, we hear the sound of hammering
                 on the C key of a piano, 3 octaves above
                 middle C for 10 beats and then the C one
                 octave lower is hit 10 times. This is followed
                 by Mary playing* Un Sospiro *(Liszt). After
                 several bars, Harry's voice is heard.*

HARRY: Mary, stop playing that fucking piano.

*The piano playing stops. All but Hago look up at the window.
Lusty laughs loudest.*

Scene 3

*At night. Outside Harry's house. Joanne, a 14 year old waif
and beauty, is at the corner leaning against a fence of
galvanized iron posts with triple spikes on top. An orange
electrical light illuminates the tableau. She has been running
and is catching her breath against the fence. She is scared
and her eyes are wild. She is wearing only a blouse and the
buttons are done up wrong. The collar is torn. In the distance
can be heard the sound of a 2-stroke motorcycle growling
louder and then fading out. On the ground are empty beer
bottles, colored glass and crushed cans, dogshit, condoms,
pieces of clothing including a pair of nylons.*

Vincent the Liar appears.

VINCENT: She's mad, she knows that of course, doesn't
            she? She's mad. She's quite mad. She's mad
            and alone. Quite alone. She knows that too, of
            course, doesn't she? She has nowhere to go,
            isn't that true?

            *(Vincent changes his voice to impersonate an
            unknown woman.)*

            Our friends Maeve and Clem...our friends
            have a place...our friends...six or seven
            years...last year...3 weeks ago our
            friends...actually January 12th our friends...we
            came back from visiting our friends...Maeve
            and Clem and I, we'd had enough of our other
            friends by then.

(Harry and David come out of the house, wrapped up against the cold on their way to go hunting. Seeing Joanne Harry regards her with hostility. Joanne looks ashamed. None of them speak. Harry and David walk on. Vincent's voice becomes one of self-satisfied disdain).

Let her if she wants to...she deserves what's coming to her... she made her bed, now she can lie in it. She never really saw them as her own kids in the first place...that's why she kept running out the door and leaving them with anybody who'd take them. The kids were like the husband...a smokescreen...they all thought he was the source of the trouble...even the kids...they all believed it... gave her an excuse to run all over the place...she was always out working or visiting her friends...gave her something to talk about when she visited her friends for a sandwich and a cup of tea...she wanted the kids if they were useful. The only way they could get near her was if they were useful. When the eldest boy, her real son, got his first job in the dairies she'd make sure she was home to make his chips and liver with two eggs on top, sometimes a sirloin steak on payday if there was one going cheap... about to turn. She'd let him take it in front of the television with his feet up on the poof...make him feel the prince...the boots from the dairies all splashed with stale cream still on him...rolling his ankles in ecstasy...sucking the soft fat out of the rind between his fingers. Then he'd hand her over his paycheck.

(Joanne leans back on the fence, her hands clinging to it. Vincent adopts another voice).

When what you can see around you has been left long enough the same way it becomes reality. All that occurs in the meantime is unreal. Sooner or later all reality is replaced by the unreal, and then we start all over again waiting for it to become reality once more. Looking back, nothing in the past was real. Reality has only a temporary place in periods of the present, and those periods are unbearable. It is better to have unreality. And so that is what we keep having.

Vincent the Liar disappears.

Curtain

ACT III

Scene 1

The yard of a dairy factory at lunchtime. Men in overalls are leaning against or sitting on the wall or on the ground eating sandwiches out of silver foil. In front of them two apprentice boys are fighting. One of them is Harry Jr., the son of Harry. The men are laughing and goading the boys. After a while Harry Jr. pins the other boy to the ground.

MAN A: Make him cry. Everybody else can make him cry.

MAN B: You're not afraid of him are you? Hit him in the head then. Give him a loaf in the head!

Harry Jr. awkwardly maneuvers his knees onto the arms of the other boy, pinning him down completely.

MAN C: Go on. Give him a loaf! Finish him off!

Harry Jr. looks uncertainly at the men then back at the other boy.

MAN D: What are you waiting for?

Harry Jr. nods his head as if building up to the act. The men laugh. Harry Jr. does it again but a bit deeper. Then the throws his head down recklessly with his eyes shut but doesn't reach the target. He comes back up again. The men erupt in laughter.

MAN A: Are you trying to kiss him or loaf him?

Harry Jr., dying of shame, looks down at the other boy, who spits in his face and escapes as Harry Jr. is wiping it off. The end-of-lunch bell sounds. The other boy runs among the men, and looks back at Harry Jr. and starts laughing.

MAN C: (*raising a mocking fist to the boy*). Go on you useless little fuck.

MAN B: (*nodding towards Harry Jr.*). Some welder he'll make Pagett. You'll have your work cut out there! He'll be no more use than his father, 'Harry the handyman'.

Harry Jr. hears this and is mortified.

MAN A: 'Harry the handyman'! He just lives round the corner!

They both look at Harry Jr. and laugh, and then walk off. One of the workmen approaches Harry Jr.

Vincent the Liar appears

MAN E: Go home and tell your father. That's the only way to get this stopped.

HARRY Jr: I can't tell him.

MAN E: Why can't you tell him?

HARRY Jr: Because he's too sick.

MAN E: You're afraid it might make him worse?

HARRY Jr: He'll die if I tell him.

MAN E: How will he die? He'll...

HARRY Jr: He'll come down here, and die. I can't tell him
             anything.

MAN E: What about your mother?

HARRY Jr: *(sniffs and pulls himself together)*. What about
             her?

MAN E: At least tell her about it. She might be able to
             do something.

HARRY Jr: I can't tell her either.

MAN E: Why? Is she sick too?

HARRY Jr: No.

MAN E: Well, tell her then!

HARRY Jr: *(after a thoughtful pause)*. She expects me to
             lose fights.

MAN E: What?

VINCENT: *(sententiously, to the audience)*. Courage
             comes from the mother, from her love and
             security, the solid base she provides.

HARRY Jr: She won't care. She wants me to fight until I
             can win all the time.

MAN E: What?

HARRY Jr: She lets me fight the other boys on the street.
             She'd laugh at me if she heard about this, no
             matter what I told her.

MAN E: What kind of a mother have you?

HARRY Jr: *(with indignation)*. She's a good mother! She
             cooks for us and goes out to work as well. It's

my father's fault for being sick. He's always been sick. I'll never be like him!

The bell goes again and we hear a voice: "Hurry up, there! Get back to work!"

Vincent the Liar disappears.

Scene 2 (part 1)

Later the same day. Early evening. The kitchen of Harry's house. Harry is dressed in a three-piece suit with a fob watch. There is a fedora on a chair beside him. He is polishing his leather shoes fastidiously. With a ceremonial flourish, he places each foot up on a shoe polish box as he sweeps the brush expertly across the shoes as part of his preening.

David stands by, watching and waiting. He is dressed up to go somewhere important.

Vincent the Liar appears holding a large pair of scissors. The blades are opening and closing.

HARRY: Now you know who we're going to see now, don't you?

DAVID: (*unconvincingly*). Bridie.

HARRY: (*spitting on a cloth, rubbing a spot*). That's right. And you know who Bridie is don't you?

DAVID: She's my auntie.

HARRY: (*with a tinge of irony*). Yeah. She's your auntie. (*He spits again and wipes a spot with his finger.*) Now, you have to stand up straight because I told her you were very tall for your age. Stand up straight.

           (David stiffens self-consciously.)

           I told her you were up to my shoulder a year ago. She'll be expecting you to be even taller now.

(David worries that he isn't even up to Harry's shoulder now.)

Now, Auntie Bridie is a good woman. She's a very good woman. You know that, don't you?

DAVID: Yeah.

HARRY: And she's very fond of you, you know that?

DAVID: Yeah.

HARRY: *(finishing off the polishing, he hurls the brush and cloth into the box with sudden contempt).* Hah?

DAVID: Yeah, I know.

HARRY: *(makes a final check of his shoes and begins to preen his trousers and jacket).* Yeah. She is. She's very fond of you. She's much more fond of you than she is of Harry even. She keeps asking me why you never go over to see her.

DAVID: *(uncomfortable, does not know what to say).*

HARRY: Hah?

DAVID: *(squirms, smiles in shame).*

HARRY: I told her I'd take you over myself to have dinner with her. She's been waiting for you all week.

DAVID: *(mortified, he can't remember ever seeing this Bridie before).*

HARRY: *(wagging a finger).* You better not let me down now, you hear me!

Harry picks up a ship in a bottle off the kitchen table and puts in into a brown paper bag, tucks it under his arm. Vincent the Liar disappears.

Scene 2 (part 2)

Outside, it's a fine evening. Harry and David set off to visit Bridie. Harry's posture is tense and it makes David nervous. When they reach Bridie's house and enter, Vincent reappears and speaks.

VINCENT: *(holding the scissors).* He always has to be doing something special, something that he thinks nobody else can do. Even if he's clipping his fingernails, he has to set up the scene like an operating theatre. Clear the table. Turn all the lights up full. Spread the newspaper out. Find the right pitch of the scissors and make each cut with the same exact slicing sound. The same pressure bringing the blades together until the loops kiss.

The blades snap shut several times. Inside Bridie's house, the atmosphere is fraught and David suspects he is somehow to blame. The house is relatively dark. David sits at one end of the sofa, Harry at the other. Bridie, a frail woman of 60, sits on a separate chair smoking in a nervous daze. Beside her on a little table is the unwrapped ship in the bottle. Occasionally Harry straightens out one leg abruptly, plucks the trouser up smartly and then pulls the sock up to its full length, wags the polished shoe and then slowly lowers the leg to the ground, releasing a sigh. Eventually he gets up and paces the floor.

HARRY: (*abruptly swinging an arm towards the door*). Right. Come on with you. Let's get you home.

David jumps up.

BRIDIE: (*coming out of her trance*). Will you not stay for a bit of supper, Harry?

HARRY: I have to get this fella home by 8. I promised his mother.

David looks confused. Harry told him they would have dinner at Bridie's house. But when Bridie looks at him, David hides his confusion.

HARRY: (*spoken with force*). Come on with you! Say goodbye to Bridie.

DAVID: Goodbye Bridie.

BRIDIE: (*gets up and goes to the door*). Goodbye love.

Bridie reaches into her apron and takes out a coin, slips it into David's hand, and rubs his hand between hers.

HARRY: Good luck Bridie.

BRIDIE: You'll have to come over and see me again soon.

Outside, Harry is deflated. They start to walk back home. Harry is plodding, looking all around him. He loosens his tie. David senses his disappointment acutely. Whatever has sapped Harry's hope David takes responsibility for as

61

he tries to cheer Harry up. Vincent the Liar watches them.

DAVID: (*acting plucky*). Thanks for bringing me to see Auntie Bridie, Dad.

HARRY: (*drawled*). Hah?

DAVID: I really enjoyed myself. She looked well didn't she?

HARRY: Hmph.

DAVID: I thought she looked well. She was happy to see us wasn't she, Dad?

HARRY: Yeah.

DAVID: Yeah, I thought so too. It's a pity we couldn't stay and have dinner with her, wasn't it Dad?

HARRY: Hah?

DAVID: Sure, we can have dinner with her next time can't we? We can have dinner with her the next time we visit, can't we Dad?

HARRY: Yeah.

DAVID: Yeah, we can have dinner together the next time.

David offers his hand into Harry's. Harry accepts it reluctantly. When he looks down at the familiar little hand in his own enormous hand he begins to inwardly collapse. But then he notices the fingernails of David's hand have been bitten down.

HARRY: What's this?

DAVID: *(frightened by the tone, he shudders).*

HARRY: Are you biting your nails?

DAVID: *(stunned silence).*

HARRY: I asked you a question: ARE YOU BITING
            YOUR NAILS?

DAVID: *(looks at his own hand splayed and held in
            place against the big palm by Harry's thumb
            and nods).*

HARRY: Wait until I get you home! (*Pulls David along.*)
            Where did you pick up that filthy habit?
            That's the most disgusting habit in the world.
            It's worse than smoking. Since when have you
            been biting your nails?

            He suddenly stops.

DAVID: *(doesn't answer, he has gone into shock).*

HARRY: Hah? Answer me! Since when have you been
            biting your nails?

DAVID: *(whimpering).* A while ago.

HARRY: *(pulling David along again).* Wait until I get
            you home! You just wait. I've never seen
            anything more disgusting in my whole life
            before. Come on! Move your ass. *('ass' is
            spoken the American way. He pushes David
            ahead of him and then kicks him in the
            backside. David is thrown forward and
            quickens his step, terrified of looking back.)* Go
            on! Get a move on! (*Kicks him again.*) Wait
            until we get home. I'll cut those nails down

for you. I'll leave nothing for you to bite ever again.

VINCENT: *(appears with the snipping scissors).* How can you hold him responsible for his deeds? 'It is not possible for any one, who has not designed his life for some certain end, to dispose of his particular actions.' No man can bear the burden of all the things he has done, least of all somebody who doesn't recognize himself in even the ordinary acts. (*Holds the scissors up.*) Everything he does is an audition for a role he has to have, but doesn't want. As soon as he perfects the role, he has to get out of it somehow.

The pair exit with Harry kicking David, who is gasping with panic. Vincent the Liar disappears.

Scene 3 (Part 1)

One Sunday at noon outside Harry's house. Joanne and Lusty are alone near where the blue tits nest was earlier. Lusty is dressed in a brown dowdy, Victorian dress that comes down to her ankle boots, and a neck halter (her Sunday clothes). Joanne is in a denim skirt and brightly colored t-shirt. On the ground near them is a whorl of dogshit. Other debris is scattered about. Lusty has Joanne pinned to the wall, her arm resting above Joanne's head.

LUSTY: *(pointing to the ground to a stone next to the shit).* Kiss that stone.

            She spits on the ground near the stone.

JOANNE: *(shakes her head).*

LUSTY: *(increasingly threatening tone).* Kiss the stone.

            She spits again, trying to hit the stone.

JOANNE: No...please.

LUSTY: Kiss it, I said. You better fucking kiss it.

JOANNE: *(cries quietly).*

LUSTY: *(spitting at the stone).* You're going to kiss that stone, there's no two ways about it.

JOANNE: *(weakly).* Nooo...

            Lusty bends down and grabs the stone and raises it up to Joanne's face. She bends down once more and wipes the shit onto the side of the stone.

JOANNE: Please Lusty.

LUSTY: Now kiss it!

(Distressed, Joanne puts her hands up. Lusty smashes them away with a downward swipe of her leaning arm and forces the stone against Joanne's mouth.) Lick it!... Lick.

Lusty starts laughing and steps back to watch Joanne wiping her mouth as the tears fall on her cheeks and arm. She tosses the stone away and picks up an aerosol canister, and takes a lighter from a little purse bandoliered to her body. She approaches Joanne with the canister and lighter held up in her hands. Joanne tries to back away.

JOANNE: Please...

Joanne slips into a pile of garbage and the filth gets on her clean bright clothes. Lusty laughs as she kicks the garbage over Joanne, as if to bury her in it. Then she puts a foot on Joanne's waist to hold her down, and leans over her with the canister and the lighter.

At the sound of voices approaching, Lusty straightens up, looks around and hides the lighter and the aerosol behind her back. Joanne gets up and stands beside Lusty, rubbing the stains on her skirt and t-shirt.

Three girls and a young mother go past on their way to mass. The girls glance at Joanne and Lusty but not the mother, who urges them on.

MOTHER: Hurry up or we'll be late for mass.

When the group is gone, Joanne falls to her hands and knees and retches. Placing a boot under Joanne's midriff, Lusty flips her over. Then she falls on Joanne and raises her shirt and t-shirt and tears her underwear. There is a grotesque struggle and Lusty slaps Joanne and jolts her hair. Joanne is no longer crying or making much sound. She is putting up a feeble resistance. Finally Joanne stops moving altogether. Lusty gets up, a little dazed.

LUSTY: *(conciliatorily).* Now, you've been asking for that. You know that, don't you?

(Joanne is relieved it's over, and to hear the reasonable tone in the other's voice. It's as good as an apology.)

You know that don't you?

(Still on the ground, Joanne remains silent. Lusty fixes herself).

Hah? Yeah, I warned you before that somebody was going to give you a hiding, didn't I?

(Joanne stands up slowly.)

But you wouldn't listen, would you? You're lucky it was me. Now, you know you had it coming, don't you? You got off lightly. You don't know what the others would have done to you...what Hago would have done to you...you've no fucking idea! Yeah, don't start feeling sorry for yourself now. If you'd really been hit you'd know all about it. Run home to your mammy now and ask her to wash your clothes for you.

She stomps off laughing, looks back a few times and then is gone. Joanne is left alone. We hear the birds singing again. In a while the earlier group return from mass, the mother urges them on

MOTHER: Hurry up or you'll be late for your dinner.

When they are gone, Joanne sits on a cavity block and gathers her knees up to herself, rocking gently, humming. She is focused intently on the ground immediately beside her, on the pieces of debris, the blades of grass, the cigarette butts, the bottle tops, tiny pebbles. She is running her fingertips along the ground and very gently picking up tiny things and feeling them, seeing if they will break apart. Her head is touching and resting on her knees most of the time. She smells her knees and lets the bristles of the tiny hairs brush her lips and nostrils. Her knees feel like her friends.

Scene 3 (Part 2)

A few hours later Harry Jr. is passing by and sees Joanne. Intrigued, he hovers nearby. Joanne doesn't notice him at first. He watches but doesn't speak to her. Although cousins, they appear as strangers.

Vincent the Liar appears.

As Harry Jr. moves nearer to Joanne he becomes nervous. When she senses his presence, she is relieved at first by his calmness and benignity. But she quickly begins to feel uncomfortable and waits for him to do or say something to her. He sits down on a cavity block beside her and starts to pick at things on the ground.

He takes a zippo from his pocket and tries to light a cigarette butt but there is no fuel. Click, click, click. *He flips the lid shut. He opens the lid.* Click, click, click *again.*

When he looks at her, she looks away and starts to rub a stain on her clothes. He thinks about asking her for a light for something to say, though he knows she doesn't have one. But he does not. He gets up and moves around and then sits down again. He does this a few times, and re-tries the zippo but it will not fire. Each time it affects Joanne a little more.

He makes several attempts to speak. His mouth opens, he turns towards her. She grows agitated and even taps her fingers against her knees. Finally she laughs.

He drops the zippo.

She gets up and walks off, leaving him alone.

VINCENT: The best days, the best summer evenings, the long evenings that took forever to get dark, the sun a big wet orange at the end of the street between the Joneses and the Noonans, sinking into the spikes of the corporation fence to keep joyriders out of the fields. On the best days he was completely alone, looking around at the emptiness and calm and understanding that there was nothing when there wasn't trouble, nothing but the sky and the air and the smell of grass if any had been recently cut or crushed by a gang. Even before the stars were out and it became chilly he would have a cramp in his stomach and a dread of what was to come and the preparations he would have to make to face the people he had to deal with.

It gets dark. Vincent the Liar disappears. Harry Jr. gets up and walks away.

Curtain

ACT IV

Scene 1

Another summer evening turning to night. Outside Harry's house, Hago's gang is gathered around a fire.

HAGO: Have you ever seen a guy taking a beating? No, I mean a beating. Have you ever seen someone taking a beating? Just taking it, not fighting back or trying to run. Have you ever seen that? Not making a sound either, just heavy breathing and the sound of the slaps going in. Well look at the guy giving the beating the next time. I'm telling you you'll never see anyone more dangerous. He wants to take out on the other poor bastard every single beating he took himself and all the fights he lost. If he doesn't do real damage the beating will mean nothing— because this guy didn't need a beating like this in the first place. He could even have been warned. The beating he gets is for something else.

(Hago pauses for the giggling to die out and all are attentive again.)

Now, have you ever seen the opposite happen?

LUSTY: What do you mean?

SALTY: They make friends.

HAGO: I said the opposite, you muppet!

Tittering.

HAGO: I'll tell you a story.

(Pauses to light a cigarette.)

I'll tell you a story. I was in a pub one time, down in Smithfield. In the horse market. I was 14 at the time. It was the only pub that would serve us drink back then. I tell a lie, there was one other place in town, on Exchequer Street. Anyway it was just me and Derek McGann. You know little Derek.

LUSTY: Everybody knows Derek McGann.

There is a gasp of awe.

HAGO: He was only that size...(*Hago puts his hand out to indicate how short, while taking a drag on the cigarette.*)...he was still that size when he went inside a few years later. Me and him were like that.

He crosses his fingers and holds them up, then pauses again and grows reverent.

SALTY: What did they put him away for again?

HAGO: What? He hit a couple in a robbed car. It wasn't his fault but they gave him life for it all the same. He told me he never even saw them. If he'd stopped the car he would've got off. But he just kept on going. That was

Derek's way.

(*He pauses to clean some shit off his shoes with a stick.*)

What the fuck is this?... Anyway we were drinking in Bo Derell's, me and Derek, in the horse market. It was about 7 o'clock. I remember we weren't in there long, we were only on our first pint of snakebite.

MEMBER 1: Snakebite!

All titter.

HAGO: That's what we used to drink in Bo Derell's. Or Black and Tans. We never ordered cider in Bo Derell's. It looked bad to be drinking cider in there. It made us look like a pair of knackers. The knackers all drank cider when they came in after the horses.

MEMBER 2: The knackers'd drink piss if you gave it to them in a glass.

All titter.

HAGO: No they wouldn't. The knackers have better taste than you or any of the rest of us. They just go mad for anything sweet.

(*All quieten down and look at Hago cleaning his shoes again with the stick, deciding whether to go on with his story.*)

While Derek is up at the bar buying the round this big guy comes over to me. He was with 2 others and they'd been watching us from the minute we set foot in Bo Derrell's. At first I thought they were the gang that caught me and Derek stripping copper off the old Buckingham Street Fire Station roof a while back, and chased after us for it. Derek hit one of them with a pole and knocked him into the Liffey.

Pauses.

Anyway over he comes, your man. Big guy. He puts his hand down on the table beside my pint. He was from around Smithfield, I knew by the look of him. He had a spot inked on the web of his thumb. 'Come into the jacks,' he says to me, 'we have to sort something out, you and me.' Little Derek at this time is still up at the bar trying to get served among all the knackers making a racket with their rolls of twenties. So I follows this guy into the jacks thinking I could sort this thing out myself. I was too stupid back then to know any better. As soon as we get inside the other two come straight in behind me.

(Hago looks around and a sudden contempt for the gang sweeps over him.)

Salty, do you like spicy food? Herbs and spices and all that kind of shit. Do you like the taste of that? Chili peppers, chives and all that shit, do you like that?

SALTY: It's alright, yeah.

HAGO: What?

SALTY: It's alright, yeah.

HAGO: Vindaloos and curries and basil and all that shit?

SALTY: Well I don't know about basil now. I couldn't be doing with that shit.

HAGO: Herbs and thyme and all that?

SALTY: Ah, fuck no! I couldn't eat thyme.

HAGO: How does anybody eat thyme?

LUSTY: Thyme's fucking disgusting, how anyone eats that in food is beyond me. I think meself it's some kind of game wankers play to see who can eat the most disgusting shit.

MEMBER 1: You might as well throw a spoonful of perfume into the soup while you're at it. It's a fucking joke.

HAGO: I can't eat that shit at all. How can anybody eat that shit?

MEMBER 2: I can't be doing with it.

HAGO: I don't know. I always thought it was just me.

           All go quiet for a while.

LUSTY: What happened in Bo Derrell's?

HAGO: What happened? Well, I knew then something had to happen. The big guy pulls a knife and starts telling me who they are and what I was going to have to do.

(*Hago's eyes open wide, his nostrils flare, and he glowers at each of the gang members one by one without speaking.*)

I wet myself. (*His mouth moves restlessly.*) I was only 14 at the time. Things like that still frighten you at that age. I knew I was in trouble.

Pause.

Then the door opens behind me. Derek comes in. The other two must have let him pass on account of being so small. He comes up alongside me and puts an arm in front of me, and pushes me behind him. (*Hago stands up and makes the gesture with his own arm.*) We're about this close to your man with the knife.

(*Addressing Salty.*) Stand up. (*Hago places Salty at the appropriate distance from him.*) Now here hold this. (*He hands Salty the piece of stick with the shit on it cleaned from his shoe.*) Your man is just watching Derek.

(*Addressing Lusty.*) Come over here behind me Lusty. (*He uses his arm to sweep her behind him, while he squares up to Salty with the stick.*) Then Derek starts walking in to your man. (*Hago walks towards Salty and suddenly grabs the shitty end of the stick in his left hand, disregarding the mess it makes.*) He grabs the blade in his left hand. And he takes a swing at him with his right. (*Hago takes a sudden swing at Salty and connects with an open palm on the face, a light slap.*)

Your man doesn't know what to do now, whether to fight back or run. You can see the fear in his eyes. He's afraid to let go of the knife, so he keeps tugging on it. (*On cue, Salty starts tugging on the stick, against the grip of Hago. There is a moment of silence as they struggle while Hago stares maniacally into the other's eyes.*)

Then Derek gets your man on the ground. (*Hago trips Salty and slaps him again to get him on the ground, both still joined by the stick*.) By now his two pals are gone. He lets go the knife to protect his head as Derek gives him everything with his right, like a piston... (*Hago pistons his fist very close to Salty but no contact. Salty releases the knife to protect his head)...* and that's his biggest mistake. Derek has the knife and he drags your man into a cubicle.

(*Hago transfers the knife to his right hand, puts it under Salty's chin, and drags him by the hair a few meters*.) He tells me to wait outside and closes the door. I can hear your man screaming inside. And I hear Derek talking to him, as calmly as he always talks, and he's saying: 'My name is Derek McGann. M...little C...big G. Don't ever forget it.' I could hear your man screaming on each letter but nobody came in to the jacks from the bar. Then Derek comes out of the cubicle and washes his hands and puts the knife in his back pocket. On the way out we look in at your man and I see him jump. There's blood everywhere. Then we leave the bar. I'm thinking Derek is in a hurry in case the pigs come, but he wants to find the other two the mad bastard.

(All laugh except for Hago.)

That was little Derek. He'd do anything for you.

MEMBER 1: Where did Derek carve his initials on your man?

HAGO: Where do you think?

MEMBER 1: On his back.

HAGO: *(wiping the shit off his hand without looking at it)*. His forehead.

Scene 2

*Harry and Joanne are in Harry's kitchen sitting at the table
at dusk. There is a pit-bull terrier in a wire cage barely big
enough to hold him. Above the cage a plaque reads:
'Department of Justice.' In the window frame there is the
silhouette of a ridge of distant hills. The smooth curving of
the skyline is broken by the tiny square outline of a house. On
the table in front of him, Harry is assembling a ship in a
bottle. On the shelf a large hunting knife is displayed. A
shotgun leans against one corner of the room. Joanne sits
unoccupied. The dog barks.*

HARRY: *(looking up from the ship to the dog).* Shut up!
(To Joanne.) I had to strip him down to a
skeleton when I first got him. Strip away all the
soft flesh and bad feeding that was on him from
whoever had him before me. He was all milky
and currish. I had to starve him for over a
week. I had to purge *(relishes this word)* him.
Then I fed him back up on red meat and raw
eggs. *(He moves his mouth grotesquely).* I fed
him minced sirloin steak and eggs and nothing
else. I made him into a fighting dog.

JOANNE: *(looking between the dog and the window, as the
dog is growling).*

What's that dot up there in the mountains?

HARRY: What? Where? That's the Hellfire Club. We used
to shoot around there years ago, in the

summer, for days at a time. It was great *craic*. It's all changed now, of course. It's a tourist attraction now. Only Germans go near the place. It's been burned down a few times. But it's been there donkey's years.

JOANNE: I think I've heard of it.

HARRY: Please God, I'll take you there one day. If God spares me. There's been a few stories about it alright. The famous one is hundreds of years ago the fella who lived there came face to face with the devil. The same thing, by the way, happened to another fella I know, walking up Constitution Hill, the far side of St. Brendan's, the mental hospital, past the Broadstone, one night years later.

JOANNE: How did he meet the devil?

HARRY: Well—(*to the dog that has barked*) Shut up!— Who? Which time now, up at the Hellfire club?

JOANNE: Yeah.

HARRY: Well, your man who lived up there was well off, a Lord or a Duke or something like that and he owned a lot of land in the mountains. He was of English extraction, naturally enough, because back then all the land was owned by the English. The Irish lived in hovels, you know, they'd no windows or gardens or anything. They worked out in the fields or digging turf— this is going back now to before the famine even. Anyway, this Lord and his cronies used to meet regularly for parties at the Hellfire club. That's were it got it's name, they were part of a club called the Hellfire club and that big old house is where they used to get together and do whatever it was they did. Nobody knows exactly what they did up there. Somebody said they used to kill animals—(*to the dog*) Shut up!—and even people, make human sacrifices and do black magic. But whatever else they did they were fond of playing cards. Your man was a notorious gambler. He'd bet on anything. On 2 drops of rain running down a windowpane. They'd have their card games all night long, all year round. No matter what the weather they'd meet up at the Hellfire Club to play cards, the Lord and his rich pals. The bets were supposed to be outrageous. One bet was that the Lord couldn't go to Jerusalem and back overland within a year. Back then that part of Europe was very different from now. It was alive with thieves and cutthroats and bandits from Turkey who'd kill you just for passing through their neck of the woods. Nobody expected your man to even take the bet, never mind finish the journey in one piece.

JOANNE: Did he win the bet?

HARRY: According to what they say he went all the way and nearly got himself killed a few times, but he made it back again alright, and won the bet. You wouldn't know what really happened, though. You'd never know something like that for sure. But it's an interesting story—(*to the dog*) I said shut up!

JOANNE: What about the devil?

HARRY: Well, anyway in one of these famous card games they are playing far into the night. It's a stormy night and the rain is pelting down. The last of the players arrived hours ago and they haven't been disturbed for a while. The Lord is down a lot of money by this time. Suddenly there's a knock on one of the windows. It's an unusual time for anyone to show up, but with the weather they could have got lost or held up. The servant opens the door and a man appears and asks to be shown in. They let him in but when he takes off his hat nobody recognizes him. He says he's a stranger and was passing in the night on foot, and needed to get in out of the weather to rest for a while, said he saw the lights from far off, and asks if he can dry his coat by the fire. They welcome your man in, the Lord especially is glad of the interruption because he's on a losing streak, and when the stranger asks them if they are playing cards for money the Lord offers him a seat at the table and tells the servant to bring him out something to eat. They play a few hands and the Lord's luck begins to change, he starts winning. Close to dawn it's the Lord's turn to deal. As he's shuffling the cards he lets one of them drop on the floor. But when he bends down under the table to pick the card up he happens to glance at the stranger's feet. But he hasn't got any. He sees instead a pair of cloven hoofs.

JOANNE: (*looks out of the window*).

HARRY: (*starts to laugh. The dog barks*). Shut up!

Resumes his laughing. Joanne gets up and goes over to the dog in the cage. She goes to pet the animal through the cage and have her fingers licked.

HARRY: Be careful now. I wouldn't do that if I were you. I told you he doesn't like strangers. (*The dog growls. Joanne pulls her hand away*.) He's after pissing in the cage now, look! He's alright, leave him. He knows there's a female in the room. That's why he did that. He just got a little bit excited by the female smell, that's all. I have him trained you see. He's not used to females— (*to the dog*) Lie down! Lie down in your bed!— It's alright, I'll clean that up later, don't worry about it. It's alright.

JOANNE: (*sitting back down*). What was the other story about the devil?

HARRY: What? Oh the Broadstone. I was told this one by Eugene Carr one night. I used to go to school with Eugene. I do see him still now and then, out walking his two boxers. Lovely man. He always loved dogs. He never married. Anyway this night, Eugene tells me, it was raining heavy and he was walking home late at night up the

Constitution Hill, up Church Street from the Liffey, on his way to Phibsboro. There wasn't a sinner about, only Eugene on his way across town. But as he's passing the Constitution Hill flats a man in a long overcoat suddenly appears out of nowhere a few yards in front of him, and starts walking towards him. As the pair of them are passing the man in the hat stops and asks Eugene if he has a light. He's polite enough and he has a cigarette cupped in his hand to protect it from the rain. So Eugene takes out his box of matches and the man steps in closer to shield them from the wind and the rain. He puts the cigarette in his mouth, then leans in and opens his overcoat to block the wind. Inside the shelter Eugene strikes the match and offers it up to the man's cigarette but as he looks down at the ground he sees that your man's standing on a pair cloven hoofs.

Pause.

JOANNE: What happened then?

HARRY: What?

Pause.

That's the end of the story. Eugene didn't say any more.

JOANNE: I wonder what happened.

HARRY: Who knows?

Pause.

But Eugene never married. I often wonder why

he never married.

JOANNE: He probably didn't find the right woman.

HARRY: I don't know, maybe you're right.

Pause.

But I always wondered why he never
married—(*to the dog*) Shut up!

*Harry goes back to his ship. Joanne looks out the window at
the Hellfire Club.*

Scene 3

One night outside Harry's house. The orange street lamp illuminates the setting and the light is on in the upstairs room. The distant sound of a 2-stroke motorcycle engine.

After a while we hear leather-soled shoes dragging. It slowly builds until Harry appears, unsteady, dressed in his suit and hat. His mouth is working grotesquely. The moment he appears, the upstairs light in the house goes out. He looks up at the darkened window and grunts. His body heaves.

HARRY: Hmph.

                (At the door of the house, rocking on his heels, he reaches into his pocket and pulls out his keys. He tries to find the keyhole, stomping occasionally to plant himself more steadily on the ground. He starts jabbing the key at the door. Finally he gives up.)

                Fuck it.

                (He pushes the bell. It is a startling, harsh ring like a fire alarm.)

                Fuck it.

                He lets it go when he rocks backwards, then locates the button again and this time leans his whole body against it to hold it down.

HARRY Jr.:   *(opens the door gently, the ringing goes on a little then stops)*. Hello Dad.

HARRY: Hmph. *(He staggers forward and raises a*

barring arm to push Harry Jr. behind him.)

Where's your mother?

He enters, and goes past Harry Jr. We hear his heavy steps going up the stairs. Harry Jr. looks out anxiously and then closes the door. After a few moments the light goes again on upstairs.

HARRY: I warned you about this.

MARY: Hello, love.

HARRY: I warned you about this.

MARY: *(scared).* About what, love?

HARRY: About what love. Yeah, that's right. About what love. About what love.

MARY: *(squeals).*

HARRY: I warned you.

MARY: *(screams).*

HARRY: Didn't I? (*A thud and sound of a body being dragged or forced along awkwardly.*)

MARY: *(silence).*

HARRY: (*quietly*). Now, where are they?

MARY: (*silence, then a scream).* Ah...Harry! (*Fades to crying.*)

HARRY: *(silence).*

MARY: Please...Harry...let me go to bed. (*Crying beginning to quieten down and then a sudden scream of pain.)* Ah Harry!

HARRY: I'm asking you a question.

MARY: What, Harry? What are you asking me?

HARRY: I asked you, where are they?

MARY: Where are what? Ah...please Harry...for God's sake can we not talk about this in the morning?

HARRY: I'm asking you a question.

MARY: What question, Harry? What question?

HARRY: I'm asking you a question.

MARY: *(violent shriek).* What fucking question?

HARRY: *(sinisterly quiet).* Yeah, that's right. Mad Mary, screaming for the neighbors to hear. Mad Mary screaming again. Big bad Harry is beating up on poor Mary again. Isn't that right? Isn't that right, hah? Go on, say it! 'Mad Mary, big bad Harry.' Isn't that right? Go on, say it... say it...go on, say it...

MARY: *(shrieking).* Say what?

HARRY: *(tauntingly).* That's right...scream again...Mad Mary is screaming again...Mad Mary and big bad Harry...Mad Mary is being beaten up by big bad Harry...go on, say it...Mad Mary...Mad Mary...say it, go on...you're mad...go on, admit it, you're mad...admit it...admit it. I'll give you something to scream about.

MARY: *(with a blood-curdling scream—he has his hands around her throat—that goes mute for a moment then returns, followed by a desperate cry.)* Harry!

Harry Jr. runs out of the house and Vincent the Liar appears simultaneously.

VINCENT: *(as somebody).* If you told somebody that, they wouldn't believe you! *(Laughs.)* They wouldn't believe a word of it.

Harry Jr. sits down where the gang had been sitting on the grass and looks up at the window and then all around him trying to put everything into place.

(Vincent as another voice). Ah, the smell of the crushed grass. But he can hardly notice it tonight because of the trouble. No wait! Hold on! He can! He notices it all the more. It's all the more fragrant tonight BECAUSE of the trouble. Yes, the wonderful fragrance of the grass is strong tonight, too strong, hideously wonderful because of the trouble. It's the trouble that brings out the wonderful fragrance of the crushed grass so strongly tonight, and makes it turn his stomach.

HARRY: Now, I asked you a question.

MARY: Oh! *(Crying and wilting in fear.)*

HARRY: *(roaring).* Where are they? *(Sounds of thumping against the wall and floor.)*

MARY: *(crying in pain, then in sorrow).*

HARRY: Now. *(Noise of something heavy being moved.)* I'll ask you once more...

MARY: No...Harry...please no. Let me go to bed.

HARRY: Where are they?

MARY: (*crying. No response*).

HARRY: Where are they?

MARY: (*crying, then a new sound, a thump, and a gurgling, muted cry that breaks into a piercing wail, some movement again, like running, falling and then back to crying*).

HARRY: You mad cunt! Call the police...go on...call the fucking police...call them...call them...call them you crazy cunt!

MARY: (*a scream and then sobbing*).

HARRY: Tell them to come for big bad Harry...go on... tell them to come and rescue Mad Mary from big bad Harry who's beating up on her...go on, call them...call them for the neighbors to see big bad Harry embarrassed by the police.

MARY: (*sound of frantic movement, an attempt to flee that is interrupted, ending in a thump and screams*).

HARRY: I'll give you the fucking police!

MARY: (*screams rise to a crescendo*).

HARRY: Get up... get over there...

MARY: (*crying*).

HARRY: Now. Let's get back to where we started.

MARY: (*moaning and crying*).

HARRY: I'm going to ask you again. Where are they?

MARY: (*sobbing deeply*). I don't know.

Outside, Harry Jr. lingers and looks up at the window. He can't leave until it ends, but doesn't have the courage to go back inside and put a stop to it.

HARRY: We'll see now what you don't know.

MARY: Ah no, Harry…no, please no…

A scream, sounds of heavy rapid thumping, falling, the scream abruptly ending then erupting again at a different pitch.

HARRY: (*roaring*). Take them off…all off! (*Quieter.*) Mad Mary stripping naked. Off!…take them off I said.

In the window their silhouettes appear. We see a gun and, at gunpoint, Mary is removing her nightclothes, the gun barrel is swaying. Harry Jr. sees all of this, panics and turns away to run then stops, turns back again and attempts to run back inside. Once more he turns away and this time he runs off.

Vincent the Liar disappears.

The stage is left empty. The voices of the couple inside the house are still audible.

HARRY: That's right, yeah…that's right…off with them…all off…every last thing…Mad Mary, hah? There she is. And big bad Harry, hah? Now you can tell the police that big bad Harry made Mad Mary strip naked as well…yeah, that's it…now you have it…

MARY: (*crying bitterly*)...please Harry...for God's
               sake...

HARRY: Now. I've asked you already and I'm going to
               ask you again.

MARY: No...please...please!

               Shrieks.

HARRY: Now you know you're mad don't you...you
               know that don't you...you know you're
               mad...don't you...don't you know you're mad?
               It's in all of you, all your family...every one of
               you is mad...the madness runs in the
               family...how could you not be mad coming
               from them...admit it...everyone knows it's
               true...you know you're mad...go on, admit
               it...admit it...go on...

MARY: (*blood-curdling screech*). Stoooopp! My head
               is going to explode!

               Deep heart-rending sobs.

HARRY: (*quietly, sinisterly*). Yeah...mad Mary...there
               she is...look at her...naked...naked and
               mad...she knows she's mad...completely
               mad...and all alone...she knows she's
               alone...completely mad and alone.

               (*Harry comes at Mary with the gun and the
               silhouettes both disappear from the window.
               Then Mary screams, the sound is muffled,
               sounds of falling, thumping.*)

               That's the last time you'll make a fucking fool

out of me!

Curtain

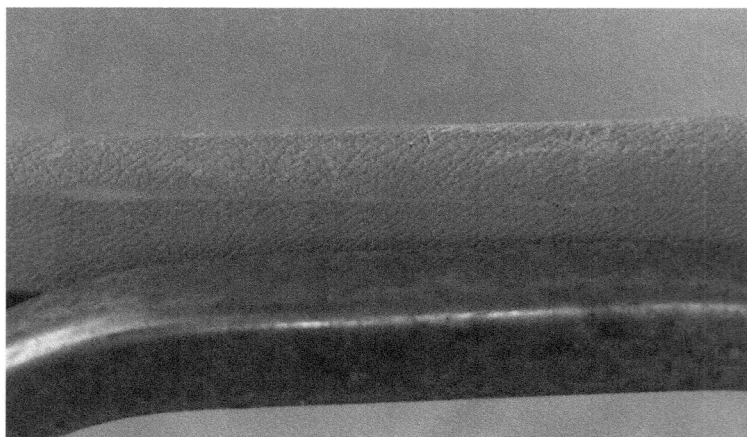

ACT V

Scene 1

Harry's kitchen. The dog in the cage is growling and barking periodically. Harry is laughing freely. The table is pushed up against the wall and on it are colored paper cups, soft drinks bottles, paper plates with iced fairy cakes and some balloons. Also on the table is the shotgun and an unfinished ship in a bottle, and the hunting knife.

On the floor is an array of brown bananas, tomatoes and grapes set out in a winding trail. There is a plastic basin in a box under the table. In the center are 4 chairs arranged for a game of 'musical chairs'. There is a group of 7 years old kids in the kitchen with Harry, all with their shoes off. The children's shoes are arranged beside the door. One of the children is blindfolded and being directed by Harry across the hazard-strewn floor.

HARRY: Alright, come on. Take a step forward. That's right. (*The kid just misses a piece of fruit.*) Ok take another step forward. That's right. Put your foot down. That's it. (*Misses it again.*) Now turn to your right and then take a step forward. That's it. (*Harry grabs the basin on the floor and places it under the stepping foot.*) Step forward. Now put your foot down on the ground.

(The kid steps into the basin filled with baked

beans and gets a fright and stumbles. Harry roars with laughter. After a few moments he removes the blindfold and lets the boy see what he has stepped in. Harry laughs again at the boy's reaction.)

OK. Who's next?—(*to the dog*) Shut up!— Who's next? (*He looks around.*) Kevin! Here, give me your glasses Kevin. Alright now. (*He puts the blindfold on the boy*.) Can you see anything? (*Waves his hands low and high. Kevin shakes his head.)* Alright! Now Kevin, here's what I want you to do, alright. Are you listening carefully to me now?

KEVIN: *(nods).*

HARRY: OK! Here's what I want you to do, alright. (*Harry takes a pair of grapefruits out of the box under the table.*) Now Kevin, what I want you to do is...are you ready now?

KEVIN: *(nods).*

HARRY: Are you sure?

KEVIN: Yeah, I'm ready.

HARRY: OK. What I want you to do is—(*to the dog*) Shut up!—What I want you to do is lean forward and kiss the object that's in front of you. OK? And then I want you to tell me what you think that object is. OK? Have you got that now Kevin?

KEVIN: *(nods).*

HARRY: OK. Lean forward now and kiss it.

           (Harry holds the grapefruits together in front of Kevin's face. Kevin Leans forward and puts his mouth against the grapefruits, and quickly recoils. Then he does it again, holds a little longer. Harry roars with laugher.)

           Is it something rotten? What is it Kevin? What was that object you just kissed? Ha! Ha!

KEVIN: *(blushes, doesn't know how to answer. He smiles with embarrassment).*

HARRY: Will I tell you what it is Kevin? Will I tell you?

KEVIN: *(nods).*

HARRY: Hah?

KEVIN: Yeah.

HARRY: OK. I'll tell you what it is so... Ha ha!—(*to the dog*) Shut up!—Ha! ha! I'll tell you what it is. It's a pair of...(*he looks around at the expressions on the other kids*)...grapefruits.

           He roars with laughter at their faces.

KEVIN: *(heaves a sigh as Harry removes the blindfold and hands him back his glasses).*

HARRY: OK. OK, who's next? Who's next? (*Looks around again.*) David! The birthday boy! OK David, you're next. Come over here and I'll put the blindfold on you. Come here. (*David is blindfolded.*) Can you see anything?

           Waves his hands low and high.

DAVID: *(shakes his head).*

HARRY: *(to the dog).* Shut up!—Are you sure now?

DAVID: *(shakes his head again).* No.

HARRY: OK! In that case we're ready. Alright now David, I want you to listen carefully to me now. OK? Are you listening?

DAVID: Yeah, I'm listening.

HARRY: Alright. Here we go. *(Harry rolls up his sleeves to the elbows and puts both arms side by side, holding them up.)* I want you to lean forward and kiss the object I'm holding up in front of your face. OK?

DAVID: *(nervously nods).*

HARRY: OK.—*(to the dog)* I said shut up!

          (Remembering the grapefruits David leans forward slowly, but before his lips make contact with flesh, he senses unexpected heat, a human smell and the contact of hairs against his face. He recoils with fright. Harry roars with laughter). OK now David, try again! You have to kiss the object otherwise how can you find out what it is? Alright now, off you go!

          Holds up his arms again for David to kiss.

DAVID: *(trembling, face red, heart racing, he leans forward bravely. Reaching the heat and hair he resists the urge to recoil, and instead holds still a moment. Then he presses on like a hero and touches the cleft of the arms with his lips for an instant, then pulls back and shudders).*

HARRY: *(roar of laughter).* What is it David? What is
that object you just kissed? Do you know what
it is?

Rolls his sleeves back down.

DAVID: *(trembling, red-faced, shakes his head only
slightly).*

HARRY: Hah? Any ideas? Even a guess?

DAVID: *(still and silent).*

HARRY: Well then what did it FEEL like? What did it
FEEL like?

DAVID: *(slow to answer, dying of shame).* It was kind of
hairy.

HARRY: *(roaring with laughter, teeth showing, face red).*
Will I tell you what it is, will I?

DAVID: *(nods).*

HARRY: Hah? Will I tell you?

DAVID: Yeah.

HARRY: *(taking off David's blindfold, addressing the
other kids).* Tell him. Go on, tell him what it
was he kissed. Tell him, Kevin.

David is mortified.

KEVIN: Your arms.

HARRY: *(laughter and a consoling tone of voice).* Yeah.
That's right. That's all it was...it was my
arms...that's all! Ha! Ha!. It was only my arms.
Silly Billy. (*Rubs David roughly on the head and*

*the boy looks a wreck– the other kids laugh at
Harry's inducement.)*

Yeah, my arms!

*(The doorbell rings: zzzzing. It is notably briefer
than in the previous scenes. Harry claps his
hands).* Alright. Time to go home now. The
party is over.

*The kids immediately go to put on their shoes
and Harry opens the door to Frank, his younger
brother, a thin haggard man of about 40. Harry
doesn't speak. He just turns and goes back into
the kitchen. Frank enters and puts his hand on
David's shoulder whispers something to him.
Then Frank sends David out the door with the
other kids.*

*Harry quickly scoops all the birthday stuff into a
large black bag, including all the stuff on the
floor. He picks up the shotgun and breaks it
open, looks down the barrel and closes it again
and stands it in the corner. He then moves the
chairs and drags the table to the center of the
floor with the ship in the bottle project on top.*

FRANK: Go straight home now, David. I'll be there in a
little while.

Frank closes the door and sits down at the table.

Vincent the Liar appears.

*Harry sits down, and immediately starts
tinkering with the ship in the bottle without
speaking. We can see the silhouette of the*

Hellfire's Club as dusk approaches. As Joanne did earlier, Frank looks frequently out of the window. After a tense period of silence, Vincent the Liar speaks.

VINCENT: Why doesn't one of them speak? They look worried. What are they worried about? Is Frank afraid that if he says something wrong his brother will dance on his head? Dance on his head like he used to do when they were younger? Or is Harry afraid that Frank will mention how he used to dance on his head when they were younger? All those years ago, but still fresh in the memory? But they can't stay silent forever. One of them will have to speak sooner or later.

HARRY: *(glancing up from this work).* The kids were mad about the gun.

Frank does not respond. Harry goes on with his work. The silence resumes.

FRANK: Listen. Don't be talking to David behind my back. OK?

HARRY: *(looking up in amazement).* What do you mean behind your back? Are you accusing me of spying?

FRANK: No. Of course not. Alright. Please...

HARRY: *(raising his voice).* No, it's not alright! Hold on a minute here now...

FRANK: *(raising his voice louder than Harry's).* No, you hold on a second, and listen to me. I'm not saying you're spying...

HARRY: (*shouting louder still*). You just accused me of going behind your back!

FRANK: Alright, forget I said that.

HARRY: How can I forget? You just said it! You can't say things one minute and then just cancel them the next! You said I was talking to David behind your back, now didn't you?

FRANK: Yes.

HARRY: Didn't you?

FRANK: Fucking yes! But that's not the point!

HARRY: Well now hold on a minute now. It is the point. It is the point. It is EXACTLY the fucking point!

FRANK: It's not the MAIN point.

HARRY: Oh! Not the MAIN point is it? Well it may not be the main point for you but, I can assure you, it's the main point for me. I don't go around doing things behind people's backs, like some kind of a snake. If I have something to tell someone I say it to their face. And that's what I expect back from other people. So if you have something to tell me, come straight out with it. Now, what are you accusing me of telling David about you?

FRANK: (*conciliatorily*). I'm not accusing you of anything. I'm just asking you to watch what you say to David when I'm not around.

HARRY: What's behind all this?

FRANK: There's nothing behind it. I just prefer if you're careful what you say to him when I'm not around.

HARRY: Around for what? To listen to everything I say?

FRANK: Something like that.

HARRY: 'Something like that'! What the fuck does that mean? Who do you think you're talking to? Are you saying you don't trust me?

FRANK: No, I'm not saying that. It's just that he's a bit young to...

HARRY: To what?

FRANK: To be hearing about guns and knives and... snakes and things.

HARRY: What do you fucking mean snakes? Hold on a minute here now...

FRANK: He told me you showed him a picture of a snake in a book!

HARRY: (*sprays saliva*). What!

FRANK: He said you showed him a picture of a snake in your book and told him to kiss it.

HARRY: Don't be ridiculous! Why would I do a thing like that?

FRANK: I'm not sure. He might have got confused or was mistaken. All I know is he was crying when he told me.

HARRY: Hold on a fucking minute now. Just back up a minute here now. I'm not sure I like the sound of any of this. What do you mean 'all I know is he was crying'? Where is he? Where is David? (*Stands up.*) I want to have a word with him.

FRANK: (*standing up*). Never mind where he is. I just want to ask you again to watch what you say when I'm not around, ok?

HARRY: I've never been made to feel so ashamed in my life! I've only ever tried to educate that boy. I would have thought somebody with all your qualifications would encourage a boy's education. I wish I'd had somebody to teach me things when I was his age. You're certainly never around to do it!

FRANK: (*sits down again*). Well...of course I encourage his education...

HARRY: (*approaching Frank*). I try to teach him about balance. For instance, I try to teach him that a hand...(*makes a fist with one hand and grabs Harry's shoulder with the other hand, then mocks a punch very threateningly*)...should be strong enough to strike a grown man and bring him to the ground when necessary. But delicate enough... (*brings the fist down swiftly but stops just short of striking then opens his hand and uses the forefinger and thumb to frame his eye*)...to remove an eyelash from a child's eye.

He leans in and lingers at Harry's eye, examining it fiercely like an eagle about to *strike, shows no sign of backing away.*

FRANK: *(finally pulling free).* Balance is important.

HARRY: *(moves away but remains standing).* Are you saying I can't see my own nephew anymore? The boy I regard as my own son? The boy who, in point of fact, calls ME Dad. Are you saying that that boy should be deprived of walks with me as well?

FRANK: There's another thing. I don't think you should take him on any more walks.

HARRY: What?

FRANK: He told me he doesn't want to go again. He told me that last time you made him carry an eel all the way back from the far end of the river.

HARRY: What? We caught an eel on a nightline. He showed a touch of fear when it came out of the river, which is natural enough for a child... *(breathes in deeply through his nose and makes a masticating movement with his closed mouth)*...so... eh...*(breathes out)*...I killed it for him...and I let him handle the river creature so he could see it was harmless, to overcome his childish fear. And that's it. *(Shrugs, palms up.)* May God strike me dead if I tell a word of a lie.

FRANK: The eel was still alive, he said, and you wouldn't let him put it down. He said you stood on it and bashed its brains out with the heel of your boot, but it wouldn't die. He said you shouted at him to pick it up...

HARRY: Shouted at him? Of course I didn't shout at him. What do you mean 'shouted at him'? (*Look of disgust.*) Why would I shout at a boy?

FRANK: He said you panicked, that you wouldn't pick it up yourself. He said you were afraid to touch it. That's why you made him do it.

HARRY: (*contemptuously*). What are you talking about? This has gone far enough now. I'll remember this the next time you come to me looking for anything...I've never felt so humiliated in all my life... and all because of a child...who'd believe that? (*In a cold tone.*) Well, that's the end of it now. When you break with me you break forever. You know my rules. There's no going back now. Once you cross the Rubicon with me that's it. No second chances. My days of being a sap are finished. I look after myself now and nobody else, no more bleeding heart cases...oh, and another thing, talking about kissing snakes, remember who was there at that child's birth while you were off kissing your boss's ass (*says 'ass' the American way*) in some yuppy conference, sipping wine and munching nuts. Yeah... don't think I forget these things...I don't forget...I'm not as stupid as you think, you know. I never forget the important things. We'll see how well David gets along now with you out schmoozing day and night and he starts asking for me to bring him out places again. You wait and see how 'scared' he is in a few weeks when he's bored out of his wits on his own. But have it your way. It's your decision. Just don't say I didn't do my best for that child. Whatever becomes of him now, I wash my hands of it. He's your problem now. You take care of him your fucking self!

Frank stares in silence for a few moments, then shakes his head and walks out.

HARRY: Adios. And don't come fucking back.

Harry instantly calms. It's as if nothing has happened. He turns back to his seat and to his ship in the bottle. The scene ends with Harry working contentedly and peacefully, a serene expression on his face. Vincent the Liar disappears.

Scene 2

An evening some days later. In Harry's kitchen, Joanne is sitting lethargically at the table. David is beside her. They are both eating cornflakes. The dog is in the cage, the gun in the corner, and the knife on the table. Enter Mary, a restless and glamorous woman with dyed-blonde hair. She ignores David, but watches Joanne like a hawk, determined to get her moving along some course imagined for her.

MARY: (*shrilly*). Joanne! Joanne! Joanne, I spoke with Maeve last night at the Clontarf Castle (*spoken with relish*). She told me Aubrey will see you next week! Isn't that wonderful news?

JOANNE: (*looking up from her cornflakes*). Who?

MARY: (*annoyed*). Aubrey! Maeve's husband's business partner, Aubrey Wills. I told you about him (*touches her hair*). Don't you remember Aubrey? Of course you do.

JOANNE: No.

MARY: Aubrey! With the summer house in Wexford I told you I went to last summer with Maeve and Grant. Well-dressed good-looking businessman. Doesn't drink. He sent me those flowers and the fancy box of chocolates for helping him at the big function at the Burlington last year. What do you mean you don't remember? The flowers were in the window for nearly a month. (*Points to the window where the Hellfire Club is silhouetted—the flowers would have blocked the view*.) They came with a special syrup to put in the water to keep them alive. 'To Mary from Aubrey, many thanks for everything you've done' is what it said on the card. No? (*Joanne's mouth hangs open and dumbly closes.*) And you ate most of the chocolates on me! I hardly got a lick. A couple of coffee creams and a few auld Turkish Delights was all was left by the time I got there. Are you trying to tell me you don't remember Aubrey?

JOANNE: Oh, I think I remember those.

MARY: I thought you would. Well, you'd better brighten yourself up and start remembering a bit more before next week.

JOANNE: Why?

MARY: Maeve says he's ready to see you.

JOANNE: See me? Why?

MARY: (*furious look*). 'Why?' Why do you always act so negatively when somebody tries to engage with you on adult terms (*'engage' and 'on adult terms' are spoken in a different accent*). And you'd better not speak that way to Aubrey after all the strings Maeve's pulled to set this up for you. You should be grateful for all that people are doing for you. I wish I'd had the same looking after when I was your age.

JOANNE: Set what up?

MARY: No wonder you've no friends! I've a good mind

to tell Maeve she shouldn't have bothered her fecking arse.

'Fecking arse' spoken with an affected accent.

JOANNE: But, I mean what's this appointment about with Aubrey?

MARY: Now, what do you think it's about? It's about work. Maeve says that Aubrey might have some work for you, and with a bit of luck it will lead to something else. Now go upstairs and put on an outfit for me to take a look at you in.

As these last words are spoken Mary sniffs distastefully and rubs the knuckle of her index finger against her nose twice. We see the nose wrinkle and the nostrils raised. There is something vile, utterly irresponsible, in this little gesture.

JOANNE: What kind of an outfit?

MARY: Go on with you, I haven't got all day!

(Joanne drags herself off. David goes after her so as not to be alone with Mary. After a while Joanne comes back down alone with different clothes on. Mary is daydreaming at the table, a strange look on her face, not really a smile but a relaxing of the face in that direction, a lapse of sorts that looks ironic. She speaks apropos of nothing in particular.)

Oh Maeve is gas, she really is.

JOANNE: *(standing before Mary, ill at ease in clothes that are a generation too old for her and out of fashion*). What do you mean?

MARY: (*eyeing the clothes*). Ah, you know. The way she is. She's gas sometimes.

JOANNE: Why is she gas?

MARY: (*forgetting she is speaking to a 14 year old, the tone is different from earlier*). You know, Maeve actually enjoys sex. (*Joanne is startled and looks around protectively for David, whom she is relieved to see is absent.*)

I mean Maeve could quite easily jump into bed with torn kickers and an old bra on her and feel no shame. I couldn't do that! She's incredible. I mean she actually enjoys sex. (*Returns to her business with Joanne*) Let me look at you. (*Looks her over, touching the fabrics with her fingers brusquely while talking.*)

Aoife had her graduation last week, Maeve showed me the photos. You should have seen the outfit she wore. It was magnificent.

JOANNE: Who?

MARY: Aoife, the daughter of Maeve's friend, Clem! Aoife's going to do medicine in Trinity in September. Maeve said she had to repeat her leaving 3 times to get the points! That's how damned determined (*'damned determined' is spoken with vengeance*) she was to get what she wanted. I told Maeve she better tell Clem that it'll be a long fecking road ahead for her—7 years it takes to do medicine—they had all

better be prepared for the wait. Clem told
Maeve that Aoife could only take boiled water in
the mornings during the exams this year, she
was that nervous about not getting the points.
Maeve said that Clem tried her with everything
but only boiled water would do. Her poor
stomach must have been in knots with worry.
God love her. But she got the points in the end,
fair play to her. And she looked magnificent for
her graduation. Now. I suppose that will have to
do. Just make sure you run an iron over it
before you meet Aubrey. Go on with you.

Joanne slumps off-stage. Mary takes a seat at the table and drifts back into a pleasant reverie.

Scene 3

An office in a Georgian house in Dublin. It is evening and through the large windows with heavy green drapes that are undrawn, we see that it is pitch dark outside. Inside is lit with soft lamps. The office has a desk with shelves behind it, a fireplace and a Persian rug and leather armchairs. On the wall are magazine pictures of models in black and white in various poses, both women and men. Standing behind the desk is Aubrey, an intensely focused and suave man in a broad-shouldered loose-fitting suit. He has a rapidly altering face and his hair is fine, lank and is brushed pack frequently with the hand in which there is always a lit cigarette. The other hand is permanently in his pocket.

He paces up and down behind his desk as if time is short. Standing in the middle of the floor facing him Joanne is dressed in her gaudy grown-up outfit approved by Mary. Joanne's stomach is doing somersaults with all that her intuition tells her about this man, the type of work he does and the kind of person he is. But there is also the vague promise of escape from her existing life and that holds her fast and draws out her courage.

AUBREY: So Joanne. (*He smiles easily.*)

JOANNE: (*her mouth moves but no words emerge. A grunt comes out instead*).

AUBREY: (*shoots her a disappointed look but quickly erases it*). Jo-anne. Is it Jo-anne or is it Joan, as in Joan of Arc?

JOANNE: It's Jo-anne.

AUBREY: Right. Right. Grand so. Jo-anne it is then. I once
knew a wonderful young lady by the name of
Jo-anne when I was living in Belgravia, you
now, in... (*eyes roving over Joanne*)...erm... (*he
takes a drag of his cigarette, swallows, then lets
the smoke out with a frown of concentration*)...in
London of course. Yah, In London. I used to call
her Joan because she reminded me so very
much of Joan of Arc—you know Joan of Arc?
She was a wonderful...excuse me...(*burps gently
and slowly, putting his hand up his
mouth*)...seamstress and you know...(*begins to
titter*)... she would come into my office at all
hours of the day...or night...and stitch my old
pants back together—I didn't have enough
money in those days for a new pair—whenever
they split along a seam...you see here...you see
here.

(*He comes around to the side of the table and
holds out a leg and, using the hand with the
cigarette, traces a line with his middle finger
from the back of the knee and up the crack of his
arse. He laughs as if what he has said is
outrageously funny. He looks at Joanne who
cannot laugh though she tries. All she can
manage is a grin as her eyes seek somewhere to
hide.*)

I kid you not...oh God! Oh God!...happy days
indeed. Ah Well! Anyway...(*he stops laughing

and shoots Joanne a disappointed look again, and again quickly erases it.) You're very quiet Jo-anne...if you don't mind me saying so. Rather shy, one might assume. No? But that's alright. That's alright.

JOANNE: (*standing very still and upright, she begins to speak apropos of something she sees but is cut off*). I've never seen this...

AUBREY: Yes. Oh really? (*Pacing and thinking, dragging on the cigarette.*) So Jo-anne, as you insist on being called. Not that I have anything against that variation of course, not if you insist...what was that you were saying Joanne, sorry for being so rude?

JOANNE: I... don't have to be called Jo-anne all the time. I...

AUBREY: Oh no? Oh really, now? How come, is that your real name or not? Do tell all.

JOANNE: No, I was just saying...

AUBREY: Oh sorry Jo-anne. Would you like something to eat or drink, I forgot to ask?

JOANNE: No thanks, I'm grand.

AUBREY: Oh, you're grand are you, Jo-anne? Well ok then. (*Sighs and expresses a disappointed look again, this time it has the quality of emerging boredom.*) Well then let's get down to business, shall we?

(*Joanne starts. Placing a hand on his desk, on some papers, the cigarette between his fingers,*

Aubrey starts chewing his lip. His hair flops forward and he flicks it back. It falls immediately again and he repeats the movement.) You've never done any modeling before.

JOANNE: *(starts to speak, but is cut off).*

AUBREY: Never mind, that's no problem. We all have to start somewhere. (*Picks up a page and looks at it.)* Now, take those awful clothes off.

Joanne almost faints. Then slowly she starts to take off her shoes. She puts the stockings together in a roll in one of the shoes. Then folds her blouse and skirt and puts them on top of the shoes. The pile is in the middle of the floor, she realizes, so she picks them all up and moves them to one side. Aubrey is watching greedily, dragging on his cigarette and tapping a foot on the same side as his pocketed hand. Joanne stands before him in her underwear like a patient before a doctor, waiting obediently for further instructions.

AUBREY: Oh, all of them.

JOANNE: Everything?

AUBREY: Yes. Everything.

(Joanne removes her bra and then steps out of her panties. She puts them down neatly on the pile to the side and returns to the middle of the floor.) Very good, Joanne. Very good. (*He comes around to her side of the desk.)* Now, Joanne, I want you to lie down on the rug. I want you to

take up a pose. A pose that you feel totally comfortable with. OK?

Joanne gets down awkwardly on the rug and reclines on an elbow. Aubrey takes a step closer. For a long while he does not speak, just stares at Joanne. Not sure what she should be doing, she continually adjusts her position and tries to think of images to keep from vomiting. Her senses have never been more alert. A multitude of unfamiliar smells swarm in her nose, attacking her. The soothing sensation of the rug against her body makes her naked body relax and feel like a foreign threat. Something is wrong but it is nothing she can put a finger on. Aubrey lights another cigarette and turns away for a moment.

AUBREY: (*suddenly turning back to her*). You don't have a problem being naked in front of people do you, Joanne?

JOANNE: (*thinks about this question, the right and wrong answer*). No. Not really.

AUBREY: Mm, that's interesting. I wonder why that is?

(*Joanne grows more nervous, but says nothing. Aubrey grows more excited*). Why do you think that is Joanne, eh?

JOANNE: (*silence, trembling*).

AUBREY: What might be the reason that you don't mind being naked around strangers, I wonder?

JOANNE: *Silence.*

Aubrey waits patiently, with a smile, for a reply

*while ogling her and dragging on his cigarette,
biting his lip. Joanne abruptly gets up off the
floor and—without uttering a word—quickly
starts to put back on her clothes in a hurry,
misaligning buttons. Meanwhile Aubrey takes a
step back behind his desk and slowly paces to
and fro, dragging on the cigarette, observing
with a calm smile, a little bored now, saying
nothing and making no attempt to obstruct
Joanne. As soon as Joanne is dressed she rushes
out of the office. Aubrey looks down at the papers
on his desk and flips his hair back with his
cigarette hand a number of times.*

Scene 4 (Part 1)

Another night outside Harry's house. The sound of a 2-stroke motorcycle engine drones in the background. In a while the sound of footsteps dragging and Harry appears, muttering to himself. As soon as he appears, the light in the upstairs bedroom goes out. Harry stops and stares up at it, then curses. He gets to the door but cannot find the keyhole. He gives up trying and leans on the bell. This time Mary comes down to answer and the opening of the door ends the deafening ringing.

MARY:	Hello, Love.
HARRY:	(*pushing past her*). Hmph.
	The door closes. Quite a while passes in silence before the upstairs light comes on. Another period of silence before Harry and the gun appear in silhouette.
HARRY Jr:	Hello, Dad.
HARRY:	Get up out of bed.
HARRY Jr:	What's wrong, Dad?
HARRY:	Get up I said.
HARRY Jr:	(*obeys. We see him standing up opposite his father in silhouette, the gun between them*).
HARRY:	Now, 'son' (*said ironically*), have I ever lied to you?
HARRY Jr:	No Dad.

HARRY: Have I?

HARRY Jr: No Dad.

HARRY: Now, I'm asking you a serious question so think about it carefully. Have I ever lied to you?

HARRY Jr: No Dad.

HARRY: (*swaying*). Hah?

HARRY Jr: No Dad.

HARRY: No.

HARRY Jr: No.

HARRY: Have I ever done anything to hurt you?

HARRY Jr: (*rising panic).* No Dad.

HARRY: Anything to hurt you. Have I ever done anything that would hurt you even one SCINTILLA (*emphasizes this word viciously*)?

HARRY Jr: No Dad.

HARRY: Did I raise you to be a fucking parrot?

HARRY Jr: No Dad.

HARRY: Well have you nothing else to say to me?

HARRY Jr: (*tries to think of something to say).*

HARRY: (*swaying*). Hah?

HARRY Jr: You've never done anything to hurt me and never lied to me.

HARRY: Right. So we both know where we're coming from here, don't we?

HARRY Jr: Yes Dad.

HARRY: Because if you don't know where you're
            coming FROM, how can you know where
            you're going TO? Isn't that right?

HARRY Jr: Yes Dad.

HARRY: Hah?

HARRY Jr: Yes Dad.

HARRY: Yes Dad.

HARRY Jr: Yes.

HARRY: Now. Here's what I want to do. OK? Are you
            listening carefully now? Here's what I want
            you to do.

HARRY Jr: (*nods, trembling with fear*).

HARRY: I want you to take this loaded shotgun and I
            want you to shoot me.

HARRY Jr: (*stunned*).

HARRY: Now. If you can't do that, I want you to go into
            the room where your mother is sleeping...and
            I want you to shoot her.

HARRY Jr: (*wets himself*).

HARRY: Now. Have you got that now. I'm going to give
            you this gun in a second and when I do I want
            you to shoot me, or else go in there and shoot
            your mother. Have you got that now, have
            you?

HARRY Jr: (*silence*).

HARRY: And if you haven't got it in you to shoot me or
            to shoot your mother then I want you to

123

shoot yourself. And if you haven't the balls to do that either then I'M going to shoot YOU. Have you got all that now? Here. Now, make up your mind.

He sways as he hands the gun to Harry Jr.

HARRY Jr: *(freezes).*

HARRY: Take it now. Take hold of this firearm like I told you and make up your mind.

HARRY Jr: *(rigid).*

HARRY: Take the fucking gun!

Harry Jr. suddenly lunges for Harry. They both fall to the ground, disappearing from sight in the window. We hear the sounds of the struggle, then Harry Jr. screams.

HARRY Jr: You fucking bastard!

HARRY: *(the sound of the Harry spitting).* Get off me!

The door opens. Harry Jr. appears and flees into the night. A little later Harry staggers out carrying the shotgun. He looks around wildly then goes back inside the house and locks the door. After a while the light goes off. In a few moments we hear the sound of snoring.

Scene 4 (Part 2)

Harry Jr. enters where the ditch and fertilizer bags are. He is exhausted and panic-stricken.

Vincent the Liar appears.

Harry Jr. staggers around and then sits down on the ground and holds his head. After a while he starts to feel cold and notices the bags on the ground. He climbs into one of them and tries to settle down to sleep. He moves restlessly. There is a distant sound of the 2- stroke engine, the sound of cows mooing and dogs barking.

A catholic priest walking through the fields alone holding a flat bottle of whisky in his hand stops to take a drink and notices movement on the ground. They resemble the movements of a dying man. The priest goes nearer and looks down at him for quite a while with a sympathetic expression.

PRIEST: May the Lord Jesus Christ protect you and lead you to eternal life.

The priest covers him up with his own coat. The cow moos. The priest climbs into another white fertilizer bag and lies down beside Harry Jr. The priest lies restlessly, uncomfortable in the bag. The cow moos. Both the priest and Harry Jr. become still. Hago's gang approaches. They loiter briefly to look for something. For a while we cannot decipher what they are saying. The priest and Harry Jr. go unnoticed by them. After a while we hear Hago's voice clearly.

HAGO: *(in medias res)*... and that's not the only reason.
          As sure as shite in a goose he knows, as well as
          Derek McGann knows, that fear is like hunger.
          When it isn't there, you can't remember what it
          feels like to be hungry. But when you're
          reminded, it feels even worse than it did the
          first time. That's why every now and then a
          bomb goes off or somebody is shot. It's to
          remind people. That's all. It's to remind people
          of what could happen. It's to build up in their
          minds and keep it fresh that anything could
          happen...

*Their voices drop to an indecipherable level and they move
off. The priest changes position in the bag. The cow moos. All
goes still and silent again. Vincent the Liar, who has looked
on but said nothing, disappears.*

Curtain

Epilogue

One year later. Early morning outside Harry's house. The rubbish has been cleared up, some flowers have been planted and the graffiti has been removed from the boarded windows. The upper window is wide open. Birds are singing. The sun is shining. The sound of Un Sospiro *playing and sounds of bacon sizzling, of crockery, of tea poured from a pot, newspaper pages ruffling.*

After a while Kevin enters, wearing his glasses. He is carrying a butterfly net and chasing one butterfly that keeps flying just out of reach. As he follows the butterfly around he uses the full length of the pole. He is utterly absorbed, and oblivious to David who appears at the window of the house to watch him. David comes down and opens the door. He comes out timidly and stands watching. After a while Kevin notices him and asks for his help.

KEVIN: Have you got another net? This one's not long enough to catch the high ones.

DAVID: (*moving closer*). What? No. We've no nets in our house.

KEVIN: I need another net. (*Jumps*) I used to have another net but it broke. (*Jumps.*) Someone broke it on me. Now I only have this one. But it's no good for the high ones, so it's not.

            Jumps.

DAVID: (*moving closer still, following Kevin*). What are the high ones like?

KEVIN: They're way up in the air and they hardly ever come down because...they're really hard to catch because they hardly ever come down low enough, so they don't...the high ones are the hardest to catch, so they are.

DAVID: There he is look! Beside you!

KEVIN: Where?

DAVID: There. Right there on the stone, he is. (*David creeps over beside Kevin.*) Here. Give me the net, will you?

Kevin hands it to him and David puts it over the butterfly.

KEVIN: Did you get him? Did you get him?

DAVID: I think so. Have a look. I'll hold the net for you, I will. (*Harry appears at the window, one arm up and leaning against the frame. The boys do not see him. The piano playing comes naturally to an end.*)

Did I get him?

KEVIN: (*heavy breathing and searching inside the net, he finally finds it*). You caught him! You caught him!

DAVID: What are we going to do with him?

KEVIN: We have to put him in a jar.

DAVID: Where's your jar?

KEVIN: I haven't got a jar. Have you a jar in your

house?

DAVID: I think I have a jar. You wait there and I'll see if I can find a jar in my house.

KEVIN: Hurry up, will you. Or he might get away.

DAVID: I'll be as fast as I can.

As David runs inside, Harry comes away from the window to anticipate him. When David eventually comes back out he is empty-handed and Harry is behind him, standing in the doorway watching.

DAVID: My Dad says that we don't give out jars from our house.

KEVIN: How are we going to keep him?

DAVID: I don't know but my Dad says we don't...(*looks over his shoulder at Harry*)...give out jars from our house.

KEVIN: What do you mean? I thought you said you had a jar.

DAVID: My Dad says we don't give jars out.

KEVIN: (*perplexed at the strange words and mechanical tone he accidentally releases the butterfly and it causes him to lose his temper*). He got away look! Oh no!

He picks up the net and slaps it down against his legs in anger, accidentally striking David and breaking the pole. Behind him Harry bristles. David senses this. Harry gives him a cold stare.

DAVID: What did you do that for?

KEVIN: What? I didn't mean it.

DAVID: (*hesitates, then looks around again at Harry and receives the same stare. He raises his voice*). What did you do that for?

KEVIN: What do you mean?

DAVID: What did you hit me with that net for?

KEVIN: (*raising his voice*). I told you I didn't mean it. It was an accident, all right.

DAVID: (*looking around again*). No. It's not all right. Why did you hit me with that stick?

KEVIN: (*looks scared, not so much of David but of the new implacable attitude. His voice becomes quieter*). I told you I didn't mean it.

DAVID: (*steps in closer, tucks his chin in*). What did you do it for, hah?

KEVIN: (*worried, his lips start to quiver, face to redden, but he says nothing*).

DAVID: What did you do it for?

He pushes Kevin.

KEVIN: (*rising panic, stumbles, is silent*).

DAVID: Why did you hit me, hah?

He pushes Kevin harder. Hurt by the second push, Kevin attacks. They fall to the ground and start to wrestle. Kevin's glasses fly off. After pulling each other's hair and rolling around for a while David gets on top of Kevin and takes a breath while the other, pinned down, lies still.

KEVIN: I give up.

David looks around at Harry then pulls his head back and drops it down and smashes Kevin in the face. Kevin screams and starts to cry. David stands up and Kevin holds his face. When he gets up, he looks at Harry and David in bewilderment, grabs the remains of his broken butterfly net and finds his glasses. He runs off, distraught. Harry emerges from the doorway and puts a hand on David's shoulder.

HARRY: In this life, David, if you manage to find a friend, just one friend—I'm not talking about a pal or a buddy now, I mean a real friend, someone you can depend on—then you can count yourself a lucky man. Very few people can honestly say that they have a real friend...*(Harry steers David towards the house)*...but if you told most people that they wouldn't believe you! (*Laughs.*) That's why, David, you always have to be careful what you say to other people. Come on inside now and help me finish the ship.

They go inside and the door closes. We hear the sound of birds singing.

Final Curtain

THE AUTHOR

George Saitoh is the penname of Gary Quinn. He was born in Dublin. He obtained a PhD in molecular biology from the University of York in 1999. He has worked at and published numerous scientific papers for private and public research organizations around the world including Syntex Chemicals Inc. (Boulder CO, USA), Institut Gustave Roussy (Paris), National Cancer Center Research Institute (Tokyo) and Novartis (Cambridge UK & Boston MA, USA). He currently lives in Tokyo where he teaches at Waseda University.

His art essays, translations, fiction and poetry have been published in *Kyoto Journal, Aeqai, Clarion, Word Riot* and *Orbis*. His plays have been performed in Tokyo and Dublin.

www.januscreations.com

www.georgesaitoh.com

www.ingramcontent.com/pod-product-compliance
Lightning Source LLC
Chambersburg PA
CBHW051833040426

42447CB00006B/506